ANVARI'S DIVAN:
A POCKET BOOK FOR AKBAR

Published with the aid of a grant from
THE HAGOP KEVORKIAN FUND, *New York*

ANVARI'S DIVAN:
A POCKET BOOK FOR AKBAR

A *Dīvān* of Auhaduddin Anvari, copied for the Mughal emperor
Jalaluddin Akbar (r. 1556-1605) at Lahore in A.H. 996/A.D. 1588.
Now in the Fogg Art Museum of Harvard University

ANNEMARIE SCHIMMEL

Special Consultant, part-time, Islamic Art
The Metropolitan Museum of Art
Professor of Indo-Muslim Culture, Harvard University

STUART CARY WELCH

Special Consultant in charge of the Department of Islamic Art
The Metropolitan Museum of Art
Curator of Islamic Art,
Fogg Art Museum, Harvard University

THE METROPOLITAN MUSEUM OF ART, NEW YORK

ON THE JACKET: Detail of Plate 13, "The Fox's Fear." Fol. 314a of the *Dīvān*

PUBLISHED BY
The Metropolitan Museum of Art, New York
Bradford D. Kelleher, Publisher
John P. O'Neill, Editor in Chief
Polly Cone, Editor
Henry von Brachel, Production Manager
Peter Oldenburg, Designer

Color photography by Clive Russ
Maps drawn by Kathleen Borowik

LIBRARY OF CONGRESS CATALOGING IN PUBLICATION DATA

Schimmel, Annemarie.
    Anvari's divan: a pocket book for Akbar.

    Includes bibliographical references.
    1. Anvarī, Awḥad al-Dīn, d. 1189 or 90. Dīvān.
2. Akbar, Emperor of Hindustan, 1542-1605.
3. Manuscripts, Persian – Facsimiles.   4. Illumination of books and manuscripts, Mogul.   5. Illumination of books and manuscripts, Islamic – India.   I. Welch, Stuart Cary.   II. Fogg Art Museum.   III. Title.

PK6451.A62Z87   1983   891'.5511   83-988
ISBN 0-87099-331-3

Type set by Finn Typographic Service, Inc., Stamford, Conn.
Printed by Lebanon Valley Offset Company, Annville, Pa.
Bound by Publishers Book Bindery, Long Island City, N.Y.

CONTENTS

FOREWORD

Of course our primary motive in naming Stuart Cary Welch to the post of special consultant in charge of the Department of Islamic Art was to secure for the Museum a distinguished Islamicist and one of the foremost specialists in the field of Indian art. To our delight, however, there were other advantages in the appointment: namely the prospect of strengthening the Museum's ties with the Fogg Art Museum at Harvard and of bringing to the Metropolitan the eminent Islamicist Annemarie Schimmel.

The present book celebrates both these happy circumstances. The subject is not a work of art in the Museum's collection, but one in the Fogg – a *Dīvān* of Auhaduddin Anvari, copied in 1588 for the Mughal emperor Akbar the Great. Furthermore, the book demonstrates an ideal for a scholarly publication: the brilliant collaboration of an art historian and a specialist in language and literature.

Anvari's Divan was produced with the aid of a generous grant from The Hagop Kevorkian Fund. Thanks to the beneficence of the Fund's trustees, the jewel-like miniature paintings and exquisite calligraphy of the tiny Fogg *Dīvān* may now be relished by Western eyes.

PHILIPPE DE MONTEBELLO
Director
The Metropolitan Museum of Art

PREFACE

Manuscripts like Akbar's *Dīvān* of Anvari were intended for handling. This copy, upon leaving the imperial scriptoria, painting workshop, and bindery, must have been received in the firm but sensitive hands of the emperor, who would have shared it with his son Prince Salim and other members of the imperial household. As part of the great Mughal library, it was enjoyed for hundreds of years. Surely its pages were turned, read, and admired by generations of appreciative Mughal rulers. Salim, later known as Emperor Jahangir, doubtless showed it to his forceful and discerning wife Nur Jahan, and one imagines it being lovingly admired by Shah Jahan and his favorite wife, Mumtaz Mahal, whose memory inspired the Taj Mahal. Ill-fated Prince Dara Shikoh, Shah Jahan's eldest and favorite son, who was expected to inherit the throne, and who was so spiritually akin to Akbar, must have admired it too – before it reached the hardier fingers of Aurangzeb, another of Shah Jahan's sons, who seized the throne. Although puritanical, orthodox, and soldierly, he, like all his dynasty, appreciated art and poetry. Presumably this precious volume remained in Mughal hands at least until the fall of the dynasty, when the last emperor, Bahadur Shah II, a sensitive poet, risked his life as the figurehead of the 1857 rebellion against the British, and lost. He must have loved this little book, and might have wanted to carry it with him to Burma, where he was exiled in 1858.

The *Dīvān*'s recent history began in 1908, when it was acquired by another discerning devotee of manuscripts, C. W. Dyson Perrins, who transmuted considerable sums of his fortune – earned through the manufacture of sauce – into a great library. Sustained, perhaps, by his varied but marvelous manuscripts, he lived quietly for a very long time. The *Dīvān* may have been his smallest volume. By the time he acquired it, along with Akbar's larger, later, and more illustrious "Dyson Perrins Nizami" of 1595, this delicate manuscript had lost its binding. Its folios were protected in a little silk bag, extremely frayed, appealingly striped in green and black.

In this condition, the *Dīvān* was offered for sale by Sotheby & Company, London, on December 1, 1959, as lot 93. It was much admired and, we suppose, stroked by more subimperial fingers than at any other time in its

9

history. Happily it caught the eye of John Goelet, the American traveler-connoisseur, who offered to acquire it for the Fogg Art Museum. We at Harvard are forever in his debt for this splendid gift of Akbar's most intimate and lyrical illustrated book of verse.

For the present publication, we are grateful to The Hagop Kevorkian Fund, which has been unstintingly generous to the Metropolitan Museum, particularly to the Department of Islamic Art. We are also indebted to the Fogg Art Museum and to its director, Seymour Slive, for permission to publish this precious manuscript. At the Fogg, I am thankful to my colleagues John Rosenfield and Pramod Chandra and to my assistants, Mildred Frost, Michele de Angelis, and Terry Antrim, for their continuing helpfulness. At Harvard, I am also beholden to Wheeler Thackston and to Brian Silver, whose enthusiasm for matters Mughal is unfailing.

At The Metropolitan Museum of Art, I owe continuing thanks to members of my department, particularly to Mimi Swietochowski and Carolyn Kane. Polly Cone has been a careful and pleasingly tactful editor.

For permission to illustrate comparative material, I am grateful to Robert Skelton of the Victoria and Albert Museum, London; to Norah Titley of the British Library, London; to Dieter George of the Berlin State Library; to Daniel Walker of the Cincinnatti Art Museum; and to the Cleveland Museum of Art.

The color photography is by Clive Russ, who worked under the sponsorship of John Goelet. Both deserve our deep gratitude.

STUART CARY WELCH

ANVARI'S DIVAN:

A POCKET BOOK FOR AKBAR

AKBAR
AND HIS TIMES

THIS UNUSUALLY SMALL MANUSCRIPT, with fifteen miniatures as fragile as butterfly wings, was commissioned by the Mughal emperor Akbar the Great (r. 1556-1605) and copied by a royal scribe at Lahore in 1588, the thirty-third year of the reign, when Akbar was forty-seven years old.[1] His son and heir, Emperor Jahangir ("World Seizer"), recalled him vividly:

> He was of middle height, but inclining to be tall; he was of the hue of wheat; his eyes and eyebrows were black, and his complexion rather dark than fair; he was lion-bodied, with a broad chest, and his hands and arms long. On the left side of his nose he had a fleshy mole, very agreeable in appearance, of the size of half a pea. Those skilled in the science of physiognomy considered this mole a sign of great prosperity and exceeding good fortune. His august voice was very loud, and in speaking and explaining had a peculiar richness.[2]

Although Akbar is now considered to rank with the Buddhist Asoka in the forefront of India's philosopher-kings, such was not the case when he inherited the very shaky Mughal throne as its third *pādshāh* (emperor) at the age of thirteen.

Not a drop of Indian blood flowed in Akbar's veins. On his father's side, he was descended from a Central Asian Turk, Timur (or Tamerlane); hence, the Mughals referred to themselves as of "the house of Timur." His mother descended from Chagatai, second son of Jenghiz Khan the Mongol — another "world seizer," whose lineage yielded the transliteration "Mughal," or "Mogul," by which Akbar's dynasty is often known. Akbar's mother was Iranian and brought a third element into the mélange of cultures inherited by the young king, to which he later added indigenous Indian components and exotic European ones in a remarkable new synthesis.

Babur, the founder of the Mughal dynasty in India, was born in 1483 in Fergana, a small principality north of the Hindu Kush Mountains. At eleven he too inherited a precarious throne, when his father, 'Umar Sheikh Mirza, fell to his death from a pigeon tower. Happily, the boy had capable

13

and loyal followers, who helped him survive a decade of struggle against the forceful Uzbek ruler Shaibani Khan. By 1505 Babur had carved out a small mountain kingdom comprising Kabul, Kandahar, and Badakhshan. When Shah Isma'il, founder of the Safavid dynasty in Iran, defeated and killed Shaibani Khan in 1510, the Iranian helped Babur against Samarkand. But Turkistan was not hospitable, and by 1513 Babur knew that his future lay toward India. When Sultan Sikandar Lodi died five years later, leaving a vacuum of power, one of the Lodi heirs, hopeful of strengthening his own forces, invited Babur to invade. Thus encouraged, Babur periodically attacked India, always unsuccessfully until 1525, when he took the Punjab. In the spring of 1526 he marched toward Delhi at the head of twelve thousand men. Sultan Ibrahim Lodi, with an army of a hundred thousand men and a hundred war elephants, confronted him on April 21 at Panipat. Babur's orderly leadership, aided considerably by his Ottoman artillery and Turkish-trained cavalry, won the day for the Mughals. Ibrahim was slain, his army routed, and Babur soon occupied both Delhi and Agra. A year later Babur defeated the armies of the Hindu Rana Sangram Singh of Mewar at Khanua, near Fathpur-Sikri, later Akbar's capital. Following a third battle, at Ghaghra in Bihar, Babur controlled all of northern India except for Bengal. In keeping with his tastes, Babur's first act was to lay out a garden. But he never liked India; nor did his Turkish officers, who longed for the cool zephyrs of the north. In his lively autobiography, the *Wāqi'āt-i Bāburī* ("Acts of Babur"), the founding emperor expressed his opinion of India with characteristic candor:

> Hindustan is a country that has few pleasures to recommend it. The people are not handsome. They have no idea of the charms of friendly society, of frankly mixing together, or of familiar intercourse. They have no genius, no comprehension of mind, no politeness of manner, no kindness or fellow-feeling, no ingenuity or mechanical invention in planning or executing their handicraft works, no skill or knowledge in design or architecture; they have no horses, no good flesh, no grapes or musk-melons, no good fruits, no ice or cold water, no good food or bread in their bazars, no baths or colleges, no candles, no torches, not a candlestick.[3]

Babur was homesick! In other passages of his remarkable work – one of the most spirited autobiographies in royal literature – his love of natural history, his directness, and his delight in the real world establish the flavor and sensibility that were to prevail throughout the long rule of his artistic dynasty. Sadly, his violent and tiring life scarcely enabled him to build upon the tradition he founded. Except for his writings and a few traces of garden,[4] little has survived from his Indian rule. It is said that when his

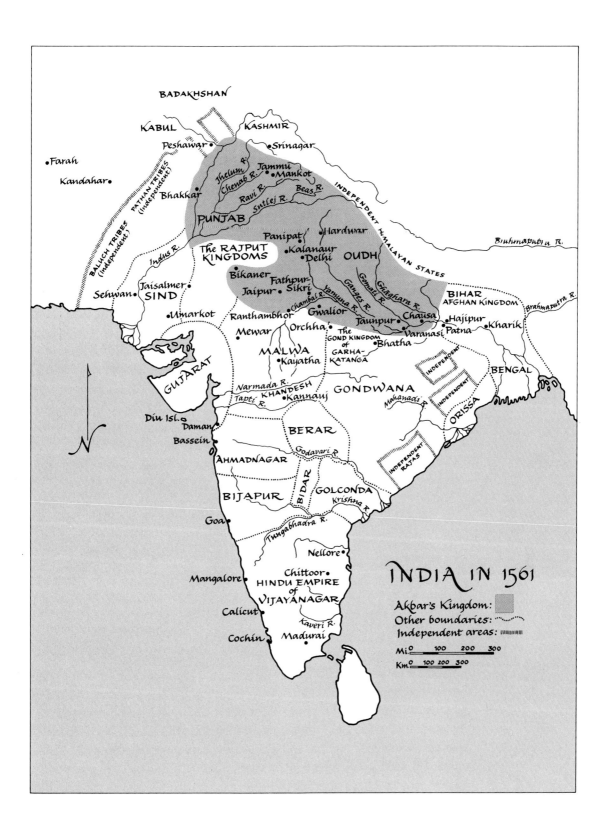

BADAKHSHAN

KABUL   KASHMIR
    Peshawar   • Srinagar
• Farah
                    Jhelum R. Jammu
Kandahar •   Chenab R. • Mankot
                    Ravi R.   Beas R.
              Bhakkar   Sutlej R.
                    PUNJAB
                         Panipat • • Hardwar
              The RAJPUT   • Kalanaur
              KINGDOMS   • Delhi   OUDH
                    Bikaner • Fathpur-
              Jaisalmer • Jaipur Sikri   Gomati R. Ghaghara R.
Sehwan •   SIND   •   Yamuna R. Ganges R.   BIHAR
                              Chambal R. Jaunpur • Chausa AFGHAN KINGDOM
          • Umarkot   Ranthambhor • Gwalior   • Hajipur Brahmaputra R.
                    Mewar • Orchha • Varanasi Patna • Kharik
                              The   • Bhatha
                         GOND KINGDOM
GUJARAT   MALWA   of
                    • Kayatha GARHA-   BENGAL
                         KATANGA
          Narmada R.   KHANDESH   GONDWANA   ORISSA
          Tapti R. • Kannauj   Mahanadi R.
Diu Isl. •
    Daman •   BERAR
Bassein •
      AHMADNAGAR   Godavari R.
                    B
                    I   INDEPENDENT
          BIJAPUR   D GOLCONDA   RAJAS
                    A Krishna R.
                    R
Goa •
          Tungabhadra R.
              Nellore •
Mangalore •   Chittoor •
          HINDU EMPIRE
          of
Calicut • VIJAYANAGAR
              Kaveri R.
Cochin • • Madurai

Independent Himalayan States
Pathan Tribes (Independent)
Baluch Tribes (Independent)
Indus R.

INDIA IN 1561

Akbar's Kingdom:
Other boundaries:
Independent areas:

Mi. 0 100 200 300
Km. 0 100 200 300

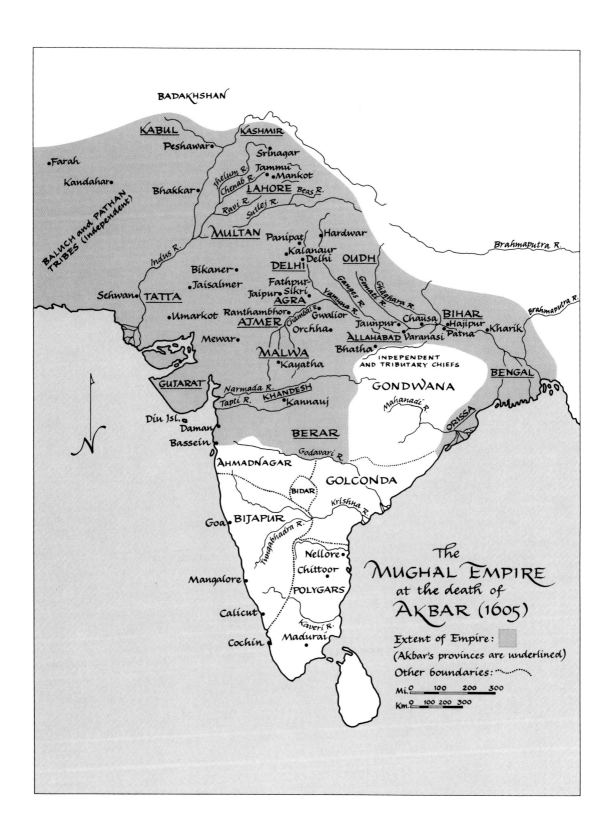

BADAKHSHAN

KABUL
Peshawar•
•Farah
Kandahar•
Bhakkar•

BALUCH and PATHAN
TRIBES (independent)

KASHMIR
Srinagar•
•Jammu
•Mankot
Jhelum R.
Chenab R.
LAHORE   Beas R.
Ravi R.
Sutlej R.

Brahmaputra R.

MULTAN   Panipat   •Hardwar
Indus R.   •Kalanaur
Bikaner•   DELHI   •Delhi   OUDH
•Jaisalmer   Fathpur-
Sehwan•   TATTA   Jaipur•   Sikri
AGRA   Yamuna R.   Ganges R.   Gomati R.   Ghaghara R.
•Umarkot   Ranthambhor   Chambal R.   •Gwalior   BIHAR
AJMER   Orchha•   Jaunpur•   Chausa•   •Hajipur
Mewar•   ALLAHABAD   Varanasi•   Patna•   •Kharik
Bhatha•   Brahmaputra R.
MALWA   INDEPENDENT
•Kayatha   AND TRIBUTARY CHIEFS

GUJARAT   Narmada R.   GONDWANA   BENGAL
Tapti R.   KHANDESH   Mahanadi R.
Din Isl.•   •Kannauj   ORISSA
Daman•   BERAR
Bassein•   Godavari R.
AHMADNAGAR
GOLCONDA
BIDAR
Krishna R.
Goa•   BIJAPUR
Tungabhadra R.
Mangalore•   Nellore•
Chittoor•
POLYGARS
Calicut•   Kaveri R.
Cochin•   Madurai•

N

The
MUGHAL EMPIRE
at the death of
AKBAR (1605)

Extent of Empire: ▩
(Akbar's provinces are underlined)
Other boundaries: ⋯⋯⋯

Mi. 0   100   200   300
Km. 0 100 200 300

heir, Humayun, was worryingly ill, Babur was inspired to take the disease into himself. He paced around the prince's sickbed, and at once began to weaken. At forty-eight, Babur died in his garden palace at Agra.

Humayun inherited the throne of Delhi at twenty-two, but was compelled by his father's instructions to yield the Punjab and Kabul to Kamran Mirza, his ambitious and troublesome brother. Worse, Sher Khan, the Afghan governor of Bihar, soon forced Humayun out of India after defeating him at Chausa in 1539 and again at Kannauj in 1540. Sher Khan then assumed the title of *shāh* as ruler of the formerly Mughal territories. At this bleak juncture, Humayun turned to his brother Kamran, who typically refused to help. Desperate, Humayun led his ever-diminishing forces through the deserts of Sind. A consolation appeared in the angelic form of a fourteen-year-old girl, Hamida Bano Begam, whom he married in 1541 or 1542. Aided by six thousand soldiers supplied by a local Hindu chieftain, Humayun led a foray against Tatta and Bhakkar. Hamida Bano Begam, now pregnant, remained at Umarkot, where she gave birth on the night of a full moon, November 23, 1542, to Akbar, whose name means, aptly, "the great."

But Humayun's fortunes otherwise remained poor. Reduced to forty followers, he crossed the mountains toward Sistan, in the hope of a hospitable reception by Shah Tahmasp, the strong Safavid ruler of Iran. Fortunately, he was welcomed at Qazvin, the capital, although the shah insisted that in exchange for asylum the Mughal foreswear the Sunni sect for Shiism, hinting that if he refused Humayun and all his followers would be burned alive. Although the Mughal's conversion may have been half-hearted, he agreed to it. Intriguingly, Humayun was sent to view the majestic Achaemenid ruins of Persepolis by Shah Tahmasp, who must have been aware of his guest's enthusiasm for art.

The history of the Mughal school of painting began at this time, under highly fortuitous circumstances. Humayun's stay in Iran coincided with Shah Tahmasp's loss of interest in painting, of which he had earlier been a brilliantly creative patron. This circumstance offered extraordinary opportunities. Without offending the shah, who a few years earlier would have been outraged by such a presumption, Humayun was able to invite three royal Safavid artists to join his entourage. Although the senior master, Mir Musavvir, refused the offer, his son, Mir Sayyid-'Ali, and 'Abdussamad accepted.[5] Mir Sayyid-'Ali was particularly admired for exquisitely fine brushwork, two-dimensional designing, and naturalistic rendering, a characteristic of Mughal taste established with Babur's deft and detailed prose style. At the outset, Mughal art differed from Safavid in its affinities to prose rather than to rhymed verse. Although the two court painters were not summoned by Humayun until 1546, and did not reach Kabul until 1549, the seeds of Mughal painting had been sown.

In 1544 Humayun was amicably dismissed by his Safavid host. Upon his return to Sistan, he was encouraged to find that the shah had supplied him with a force of fourteen thousand horsemen with which to capture the strategic fort of Kandahar, now held by one of Humayun's brothers, who surrendered it in 1545. The Safavis looted the fort and sent the spoils to Shah Tahmasp. Humayun, however, surprised the Safavid garrison and captured Kandahar for himself, with the object of using it as a base from which to attack Kabul, currently in the hands of his most treacherous brother, Kamran Mirza.

Forewarned, Kamran fled; in November 1545 Humayun entered Kabul unopposed. There, at last, he was reunited with Hamida Bano Begam and Prince Akbar. On the advice of astrologers, Akbar was circumcised and given an additional, more auspicious, name, Jalaluddin ("Majesty of Religion") to precede his others, Muhammad Akbar. To ensure improved fortunes, he was also assigned a new birthdate.

When Akbar was five, in November 1547, his first of a series of tutors was appointed. None of the prince's teachers was able to direct the headstrong pupil away from such outdoor activities as pigeon flying or from swordsmanship and other martial arts. It is believed that Akbar never learned to read or write, perhaps because he did not need to.[6] There was always someone at hand to read aloud to him, and he possessed an amazingly retentive mind as well as universal curiosity. His memory was doubtless enhanced by his illiteracy. It is said that he knew the names of his thousands of horses, elephants, and pigeons as well as those of his vast entourage of soldiers, administrators, artists, and craftsmen. Moreover, even as a young child, he enjoyed being read to from a rapidly expanding library. As a boy he learned by heart verses by such mystical poets as Hafiz and Jalaluddin Rumi.

During the ongoing years of exile, Humayun continued to be tormented by his poetically talented but villainous brother Kamran, who recaptured Kabul in 1547, abducting Akbar in the process. Vicious by nature, Kamran tortured many of Humayun's followers, and, when the emperor laid siege to the fort, the rebel silenced the Mughal guns by exposing Prince Akbar to their fire. Despite such nastiness, Humayun continued to forgive Kamran, who persisted in raiding and plundering until 1553, when he was again captured and handed over to Humayun. Against the advice of his councillors, Humayun spared his brother's life, but Kamran was reduced to harmlessness by being blinded, a horrible operation that the Mirza suffered with admirable fortitude. He was then permitted to leave for a pilgrimage to Mecca, where he died three years later.

In 1551, when another of Humayun's brothers, Hindal, was slain in a skirmish, Ghazna, which he had ruled, was awarded as a fief to Prince Akbar. The young prince was married, at the age of nine, to this late uncle's daughter.

From his temporary capital at Kabul, Humayun laid plans for the recapture of India. Islam Shah Sur, the capable son of Sher Shah Afghan, who had driven Humayun from India, died in 1554 and was succeeded by Muhammad Adili Shah, a less dangerous opponent. In mid-November 1554 Humayun took a raft down the Kabul River to Peshawar and later crossed the Indus. A ceremony was then held to seek a divine blessing on the undertaking. Twelve-year-old Akbar was solemnly read verses from the Koran, with each reading followed by ritual breathing upon the son by his father.

The combination of military and spiritual forces proved effective. By February 1555 Humayun had taken Lahore, and on June 22 the Mughal armies scored a decisive defeat over Sikandar Sur at Sirhind. The victory was ascribed to Akbar, who was at once declared heir apparent. In July Humayun was reinstalled on the throne of Delhi.

Akbar, at twelve, was appointed governor of the Punjab, and one of his father's leading generals, Bairam Khan, was named his guardian. Hunting and soldiering continued to be Akbar's favorite pursuits, the latter activity directed against Sikandar Sur, who continued to claim the throne of Hindustan. While the prince and his guardian were campaigning at Kalanaur, terrible news was brought from Delhi. On January 24, 1556, Humayun had been visiting his library when the sunset call to prayer sounded. Startled, he had tripped on a slippery stone and fallen down the staircase, fracturing his skull. He had never regained consciousness and had died three days later. The tragedy was kept secret by such means as a double appearing in Humayun's place. On February 14, 1556, thirteen-year-old Akbar was enthroned on a makeshift brick platform at Kalanaur.

The boy emperor's domains, however, were distressingly vulnerable, and his future precarious. His armies consisted of little more than Bairam Khan's battalion in the Punjab; the government was chaotic, and famine rife. The Sur family still threatened, and Hemu, a Hindu general who had proclaimed himself king, offered an additional challenge. Akbar's territories were hemmed in by rivals. To the north, Kashmir, Sind, and other lesser states were fully independent. Kabul, nominally in the hands of Akbar's younger brother, also demanded watching, while to the east Bengal, an independent kingdom for two generations, was as potentially menacing as the Rajput princedoms of Rajasthan. Had these Hindu clans united, they could have ended Akbar's rule at the start. In central India, Malwa was also independent, along with Gujarat, Orissa, and the many wild tribal areas held by India's aborigines. Southward, in the Deccan, the sultans of such states as Bidar, Ahmadnagar, Golconda, and Bijapur must have considered the Mughals pretentious upstarts. Further south, the Hindu rulers of Vijayanagar commanded a vast stretch, while Portugal, unrivaled in seapower, held such ports as Goa. Young Akbar's challenges were immense.

Indeed, the "empire's" primary asset was the young Emperor Akbar. Fortunately, the prince was being loyally and intelligently protected by Bairam Khan, who intuitively knew the dynamic boy's personality and needs. As before, Akbar sponged up information from experience as well as from books, which he continued to learn from by ear if not by eye. During campaigns and hunts, coffers of books as well as official records were part of his equipage. Already, it seems, Akbar was aware of one of his life's guiding principles, that a wise *pādshāh's* zeal for territorial expansion must be unrelenting. Long stretches of Akbar's early years as emperor were spent in the field of battle and in stabilizing his conquests.

Perhaps the most important battle in Mughal history, the one that elevated the dynasty to its position as a major power, was the second battle of Panipat, in which Akbar and Bairam Khan defeated Hemu, who now called himself Raja Bikramajit. Although the enemy foot soldiers, elephants, and horsemen outnumbered those of the Mughals, the struggle ended when Hemu was skewered through an eye by an arrow. He lost consciousness, and his elephant fled the field, following which his leaderless forces scattered. The unconscious but still living Hindu was lugged before Bairam Khan, who delivered the death blow, after failing to persuade Akbar to earn the title *ghāzī* ("slayer of the infidel") by bloodying his sword on the wounded prisoner. The victory was followed by a march to Delhi, which Akbar entered in triumph. Agra also capitulated, and there Hemu's old father was executed. The traditional tower of severed heads was erected in celebration.

These were rugged, energetic, often brutal times. Within a month, Akbar and Bairam Khan were again in the field, against Sikandar Sur, who finally surrendered at Mankot, in the Punjab hill state of Jammu. A wise precedent was now established, one that eased the pain of defeat by the Mughals. Instead of being executed or imprisoned, Sikandar was awarded the *jāgīrs* (fiefs) of Kharid and Bihar.

By 1560, when Akbar was eighteen, his domains included the great fortress of Gwalior in central India and Jaunpur in the east. But Akbar, now a mature young man, chafed under the domination of Bairam Khan, whose loyalty and strength, so welcome earlier, now became aggravations. Arrogant and mercenary, the old general was no longer indispensable. Encouraged by his mother, his stepmother, and other ladies of the imperial household, Akbar tactfully informed Bairam Khan of his need for independence and urged him to go to Mecca on a pilgrimage. Obediently, the regent returned his insignia to Akbar; but then, angered by his erstwhile charge's seeming disloyalty, he rebelled. He was soon captured in the Punjab hills and brought before the emperor, who generously forgave him and arranged for the trip to Mecca. En route, in Gujarat, Bairam was murdered by long-standing enemies. His four-year-old son, 'Abdurrahim, later one of Akbar's foremost generals as well as a notable poet and patron of painting, was summoned to court, where Akbar took charge of his education.

Freed from his hampering regent, Akbar now faced a subtler hazard, the petticoat intrigue of a favorite foster mother, Maham Anaga, who plotted on behalf of her erratic son, Adham Khan. He was appointed commander of a campaign against Baz Bahadur, the poetically minded ruler of Malwa, remembered for his idyllic love affair with Rupmati. After taking Malwa in 1561, instead of sending on the choicest spoils to Akbar, Adham Khan passed on a few elephants, but kept the women and treasure for himself. Akbar was offended, and his ire became outrage when he learned that Adham Khan had butchered Malwa's innocent citizenry. Impetuous by nature, Akbar sped with a small escort to Malwa, where he confronted his ill-starred commander. The emperor's admiring official biographer, Abu'l-Fazl 'Allami, described the scene in his fulsome *Akbarnāma* ("Story of Akbar"): "When [Adham Khan's] eye fell on the world-illuminating beauty of His Majesty... he became confounded, and like a bewildered moth dismounted and did homage. He placed the face of servitude in the dust of supplication and was exalted by kissing the stirrup."[7] Nevertheless, he persisted in his follies, spurred on by Maham Anaga and a few others at court. The emperor withheld firm action, but kept watch. In 1562, Adham Khan lost control of his temper. Distressed by Akbar's appointment of Muhammad Atga Khan as minister, Adham and two accomplices broke into a meeting and mortally wounded the Atga, who staggered into the adjoining courtyard and expired. Awakened by the commotion, Akbar rushed from his chamber to confront the now desperate murderer. Adham Khan impertinently grabbed the emperor's sword, at which Akbar knocked him out with his fist. Still furious, he ordered attendants to bind the villain and toss him into the courtyard below, a deed that required repetition to end Adham Khan's life. The episode was illustrated in Akbar's own copy of the *Akbarnāma.* This impressive miniature includes a vital but dignified portrait of Akbar at the age of twenty-one (Figure 1). Although Maham Anaga admitted to Akbar that he had done the right thing, her intrigues ended only forty-six days after Adham's death, when she herself died. Akbar built the overly devoted mother and her disturbingly ambitious son a superb tomb near the Qutb Minar. It is still visited by admiring tourists, few of whom know of its dramatic origins.

During these early years of his reign, Akbar overflowed with physical energy, which he released spontaneously, at times recklessly, as in the episode involving a vast elephant named Hawai, or "Skyrocket," probably the animal ridden by Hemu at the time of his defeat and noted for its "choler, passionateness, fierceness, and wickedness," according to Abu'l-Fazl. After a few cups of wine, Akbar alarmed his companions by mounting this earthquake of a mammal and executing "wonderful manoeuvres." But these were a mere prelude to his next antic – challenging another hulking elephant, Ran Bagha ("Tiger in Battle"), to combat. Such contests, an imperial prerogative in Mughal India, too often led to the deaths of the *mahouts,* or elephant drivers, daring men trained in this specialty and usually assigned for years to a single elephant. An emperor thus risking his life was unheard of, but Akbar directed ferocious Hawai at Ran Bagha, who fled past horrified witnesses toward the banks of the Yamuna River, hotly pursued by Akbar on his "rocket." Ran Bagha plunged across a bridge of boats, swamping them, and was still followed by Hawai and the determined imperial *mahout.* Once across, Ran Bagha rushed for shelter, and Akbar swiftly brought the outraged Hawai under control.[8]

Akbar was infallibly and unself-consciously aware of his potential. Like a magnet, he drew all and everything toward himself, from territories to gold, jewels, poets, artists, theologians, and ideas. People fascinated him, and he them. He knew innately whom he could put to what task. After entrancing people with his charisma, he seemed to transmute their personalities, empowering them with extra vitality and inspiring them to serve his vision of the Mughal state. Like some wizardly engineer, Akbar brought together the essential elements of his empire, a hotch-potch of people, lands, and ideas comparable to the cogs, nuts, and bolts from which only he could assemble a wondrously intricate machine. It was so well

FIGURE 1. Adham Khan Being Thrown from the Wall at Agra. From the *Akbarnāma,* Victoria and Albert Museum, London. I.S. 2-1896, 29/117.

planned that it functioned with might and efficiency until his death in 1605. Not quite a solution to the problem of perpetual motion, this astonishing whirligig of an empire nonetheless survived into the eighteenth century, after which it carried on, clanking and sputtering, until 1858, when the British exiled the last Mughal emperor to Burma.

In Akbar's India, everyone and everything served the empire, which could be interpreted as an extension of the emperor's being. It grew to be as vast as the imperial ego, including all of Hindustan and more: Malwa (1562); Chittoor (1568); Ranthambhor and Kalanjar in Bundelkhand (1569); Gujarat (1573); Bengal (1576); Kashmir (1586); Sind (1591); part of Orissa (1592); Baluchistan and Makran (1594); Kandahar (1595); and Berar, Khandesh, and part of Ahmadnagar (1595-1601).

Word spread of Akbar's expanding empire and the need to staff its growing offices, barracks, workshops, hospitals, schools, and places of worship. Men of talent flocked to the court, eager for employment by the creative and bountiful young ruler. Bartoli, a European visitor, wrote that Akbar was "great with the great; lowly with the lowly." He was also described as "unusually pleasant and serene," with "eyes that sparkled like the sea in sunshine." Not one for rigid protocol, unlike most later Mughal emperors, he enjoyed working side by side with craftsmen, from matchlock makers to cannon founders and painters.

Some intriguing details of Akbar's habits and personality are known. As might be expected of one so physically endowed, he was an accomplished drummer. Ordinarily he slept no more than three hours each night. Among his favorite fruits were grapes, melons, and pomegranates, which he often ate with opium and wine. The latter, doubtless, fired his impetuosity, as when he challenged his own sword to a fight; he might have killed himself by rushing at the blade had an anxious courtier not risked his own life by butting the sword aside and slightly wounding the infuriated Akbar. Unconventional, the emperor defied many accepted ways. In India it was the custom to conduct war in the cool season only, and more than once Akbar surprised enemies by rapid marches through heat or rain. Often he prepared for military campaigns by great hunting parties. If some victories resulted from his spontaneous bursts of might, others were earned by Akbar's own careful planning, down to the last logistic detail.

His armies must have resembled a curious circus on the move – an endless procession of war elephants, camels, mules, horses, bullock carts, goats, soldiers, and camp followers. Merchants accompanied the army, selling provisions at strictly controlled prices. Life in the field, whether for hunting or fighting, brought considerable excitement and pleasure as well as risk. Colorful tents, drumming and other military music, recitations of heroic poetry, banquets, dancing girls, and lively conversation assuaged the heat and dust. Everyone except the senior members of the harem seems to have participated in such ventures, which were vividly sketched for the *Akbarnāma* by artists in the entourage.

Religion ranked high among Akbar's all-encompassing curiosities. As a child he memorized mystical verse; at fifteen, during the course of a solitary and death-defying adventure with a notoriously unmanageable horse, he dismounted and "assumed the posture of communing with his God." In his late twenties, eager for an heir, he made repeated pilgrimages on foot to the shrine of a well-known saint of the Chishti order at Ajmer; and in 1575, at thirty-three, he ordered the building of the ʿibādat-khāna, a special house for religious discussions, at his capital, Fathpur-Sikri. At first the spiritual meetings or debates were limited to Muslims of various sects and degrees of orthodoxy; but later they included Hindus, Jains, Parsis, and Christians.

Akbar was a genuine visionary and a serious religious devotee. Both Abu'l-Fazl and Badaoni, the extremely orthodox Muslim who often disapproved of Akbar's religious eccentricities, wrote at length about the emperor's approach to God. But Badaoni was surprisingly sympathetic to Akbar's devotion:

> His Majesty spent whole nights in praising God; he continually occupied himself in pronouncing *Yā huwa* ["O He" (God)] and *Yā Hādī* ["O Guide"], in which he was well versed. His heart was full of reverence for Him, who is the true Giver, and from a feeling for his past successes he would sit many a morning in prayer and meditation on a large flat stone of an old building which lay near the palace in a lonely spot, with his head bent over his chest, gathering the bliss of the early hours of dawn.[9]

Akbar's knowledge and use of such repeated formulas, known as *dhikr* to Muslims and *mantras* to Hindus and Buddhists, is but one instance of his attention to religious disciplines. In 1583 the emperor's religious explorations sparked less laudatory but equally interesting remarks from the same author:

> His Majesty even learned alchemy, and showed in public some of the gold made by him. On a fixed night, which came once a year, a great meeting was held of Jogis [Hindu ascetics] from all parts. This night they called *Sivrāt*. The Emperor ate and drank with the principal Jogis, who promised him that he should live three or four times as long as ordinary men. His Majesty fully believed it, and connecting their promises with other inferences he had drawn, it became impressed on his mind.... Fawning court doctors, wisely enough,

found proofs of the longevity of the Emperor, and said that the cycle of the moon during which the lives of men are short was drawing to its close, and that...with a new cycle...the original longevity of mankind would again commence. Thus, they said, it was mentioned in some holy books that men used to live up to the age of one thousand years; and in Thibet there was even now a class of *Lāmahs*, or devotees, and recluses, and hermits of Cathay, who live two hundred years, and more. For this reason His Majesty, in imitation of the usages of those *Lāmahs*, limited the time he spent in the Haram, curtailed his food and drink, but especially abstained from meat. He also shaved the hair of the crown of his head, and let the hair at the sides grow, because he believed that the soul of perfect beings, at the time of death, passes out by the crown...with a noise resembling thunder, which the dying man may look upon as proof of his happiness and salvation from sin, and as a sign that his soul by metempsychosis will pass into the body of some grand and mighty king.[10]

At the age of thirty-six at Bhera in the Punjab, Akbar, to quote Abu'l-Fazl, experienced "what the chiefs of purity and deliverance [holy men] had searched for in vain." He "saw the light," an event far from unique, which usually occurs to people of deep religious sensibility in their late thirties, although the details vary considerably.[11] In Akbar's case, two contrasting activities had gone immediately before the experience: a visit to the tomb of a saint and the preparations for a grand *qamurgāh*, a sort of hunt developed by the Mongols in which animals from miles around were driven into a fenced enclosure by beaters, then horribly slaughtered. Revulsed by the prospect of such mass killing, Akbar stopped the hunt, to the astonishment of his entourage, who had spent ten days readying for it. According to Abu'l-Fazl, Akbar "made every endeavour that no one should touch the feather of a finch and that they should allow all the animals to depart according to their habits." Then, while Akbar was sitting beneath a tree like the Buddha, "the lamp of vision became brilliant. A sublime joy took possession of his bodily frame. The attraction of cognition of God cast its ray."[12] Even Badaoni was impressed: "All at once a strange state and strong frenzy came upon the Emperor, and an extraordinary change was manifested in his manner, to such an extent as cannot be accounted for. And everyone attributed it to some cause or another; but God alone knoweth secrets." Badaoni then quoted these lines of verse:

Take care! For the grace of God comes suddenly,
It comes suddenly, it comes to the minds of the wise.

Following the vision, "at the foot of a tree that was then in fruit, [Akbar] distributed much gold to the faqirs and poor, and laid the foundation of a lofty building, and an extensive garden at that place."[13] He also cut off his hair, which he had grown long in Hindu style, suggesting that now more than ever he could be wholly himself, oblivious to others' expectations. Despite the profundity of his revelation, Akbar returned at once to worldly considerations and made a decision regarding land boundaries. But on his return to Fathpur-Sikri, he released his religious emotion by filling a large pool in the palace courtyard with coins, a benefaction so generous that it took three years for distribution.[14]

Akbar's approach to religion as a statesman, as opposed to his personal experience of God, was an aspect of his scheme of empire. Realizing that India's plethora of religions and sects divided her people, he strove to promote religious toleration – at times with success, but often with results that even now stir controversy. In 1563, at twenty-one, he rescinded the pilgrim tax, thus removing a thorn from the sides of many of his people. The following year he took a more aggressive step by abolishing the *jizya*, or poll tax, on all non-Muslims, which had burdened especially Hindus, Parsis, and Jains.[15] Orthodox Muslims like Badaoni were increasingly distressed by Akbar's religious policies, and one can imagine the outrage the official scribe felt when ordered by the autocratic emperor to translate a Hindu religious epic into Persian to promote fuller understanding of Hinduism among Muslims. Two of Akbar's greatest surviving manuscripts are the brilliantly illustrated copies, now in Jaipur, of the *Rāmāyana* ("Story of Rama") of 1588 and the *Razmnāma* ("Book of Wars"), a translation of the *Mahābhārata* completed in about 1586.[16] *Krishna Lifts Mount Govardhan* (Figure 2) of about 1590, from a copy of the *Harivamsá* ("Genealogy of Hari"), is a superb, closely related example from one of the emperor's Persian translations of a Hindu epic.[17]

Noting Akbar's semi-vegetarianism, his edicts against the slaughter of cows, sacred to Hindus, and his appointments of Hindus to prominent posts, some Muslims wondered if their emperor did not favor Hindus over those of his own faith. Abu'l-Fazl's unquestioning, indeed strongly supportive, writings about Akbar's religious policies, as well as Badaoni's biased remarks, provide strong arguments for either interpretation. All reveal, however, that Akbar's most extreme religious scheme – the Din-i Ilahi, or Divine Faith, an eclectic, elite religious order intended to bring together adherents of all faiths – was a dismal failure due to the lack of followers. Although the emperor was usually tolerant of even the more extreme Hindus and Muslims, incidents could be cited to "prove" his animosity to either, or both. In all likelihood, he remained a Muslim and died in that faith.

An important factor in the development of Akbar's reign is its coincidence with the turn of the first millennium of the Islamic era. Chiliastic

movements had been in the air since the late fifteenth century. The most important was that of the so-called Mahdi of Jaunpur, Sayyid Miran Muhammad, who was generally acknowledged as a man of extreme piety, an ascetic with a strong bent toward mysticism, who stressed the absolute importance of *dhikr* in the lives of his followers. He is said to have declared himself to be the promised mahdi, and, despite the friendship of Sultan Mahmud Begra of Gujarat, he was persecuted by the orthodox and died in 1505 at Farah in Afghanistan. His followers were found in Gujarat, Sind, and the Deccan, and a number of leading figures of the sixteenth century were either mahdawis themselves or had close connections with the movement. One with close connections to Akbar was Sheikh Mubarak of Nagore, father of the court poet Faizi and of Abu'l-Fazl. Another was Qadi Qadan of Sehwan, the first known poet of Sindi mystical verse, whose grandson was Mian Mir of Lahore, the religious preceptor of Akbar's great-grandson, Dara Shikoh. Even Badaoni wrote with highest praise of the religious zeal of the mahdawis. Although they were cruelly persecuted during the Suri interregnum, their tenets remained a strong undercurrent in religious life. Their ideas of a mahdi who would appear at the end of time and of a *mujaddid*, or reformer, for the new century and even more for the new millennium, may have inspired Akbar, Abu'l-Fazl, and his family with notions that seemed dangerous to orthodox Muslims.

Also religiously significant during Akbar's reign was the Raushaniyya movement, which sprang up in the Pathan areas, led by Bayezid Ansari, known as Pir-i Raushan, the "luminous master"– or as Pir-i Tarik, the "dark master," to his enemies. His movement seems also to have been mystically motivated and possibly to have contained some tendencies found in the Ismaili tradition, which was alive in the eastern parts of Iran and in the Hindu Kush. In any case, Pir-i Raushan was the first to compose religious literature in his native idiom, Pashto. Akbar's attempt to silence the movement by strong military action was more likely due to his fear of Pathan rebelliousness than to the content of the Pir's mystical message.

Another powerful religious personality of the period was Muhammad Ghauth Gwaliori, the spiritual guide of Akbar's greatest musician, Tansen. His brother, Sheikh Phul, had been Humayun's adviser and was therefore killed by Prince Hindal, who feared his power. Later, Muhammad Ghauth tried to impress Akbar, but without success. His work, *Jawāhir-i khamsa* ("The Five Jewels"), is a most interesting combination of Sufi thought,

FIGURE 2. Krishna Lifts Mount Govardhan to Protect His Followers from Indra's Wrath. From the *Harivamsá*, The Metropolitan Museum of Art, New York. Purchase, Edward C. Moore, Jr. Gift, 1928: 28.63.1.

astrology, and magic. It is still widely read in the subcontinent. Ironically, the idea of a "reformer of the second millennium" was taken up by Akbar's most outspoken critic, Ahmad Sirhindi, who saw himself as the leader who had come to purify Islam of the un-Islamic accretions brought in by Akbar.

Much of Akbar's success as a leader depended upon his empathy with people. Although he could be impetuously cruel, as when he ordered a negligent night watchman thrown from the ramparts, he abhorred suffering. He abolished involuntary *suttee*, the Hindu rite in which widows burned themselves alive on their husbands' funeral pyres. In 1583, upon learning that a widow was about to be compelled to carry out this self-sacrifice, he scurried to save her. Presumably, much of Akbar's understanding of Hinduism was gained in his harem, a virtual separate township of five thousand inhabitants, supervised by a special team of women and protected from without by a regiment of eunuchs, backed by a force of Rajputs. Many of Akbar's wives were Hindus, including the eldest daughter of Raja Bihar Mal of Amber, whom he married in 1562, and who was the mother of Prince Salim, Akbar's successor, better known as Emperor Jahangir. One of the emperor's greatest generals, Raja Man Singh, a member of the same royal house, joined the imperial court at this time. Whether or not the emperor's marriage was politically motivated, it was happy, and it led to further marriages between Akbar and women from other distinguished and powerful Rajput clans. In 1570, for instance, Akbar married princesses of both Bikaner and Jaisalmer, thereby gaining further military support from Rajasthan, for the Rajputs were of the Kshatriya caste of Hindus, specialists in government and warfare.

A glance at the illustrations to Akbar's *Dīvān* of Anvari informs us of a few of the roles of women at his court, particularly dancing girls and other entertainers. One cannot imagine ladies of Akbar's harem wandering about unprotected as in *Ladies Witnessing Suggestive Donkeys* (Plate 11); and the manuscript contains no portrayals of senior wives or widows, such as Hamida Bano Begam, who must have been a dignified matronly figure. Although a wife's position in Mughal India was extremely constrained in comparison to her place in our society, and she did not ordinarily attend court functions, it was possible for her to wield considerable power "behind the throne." She was also in a position to gather considerable wealth – and to spend it. When Hamida Bano Begam died, forty-eight years after Humayun, she left behind a large treasure store in her house, with the request that it be divided among her male descendants. Of women as consumers, Abu'l-Fazl has this to say:

On the third feast-day of every month, His Majesty holds a large assembly for the purpose of inquiring into the many wonderful things found in this world. The merchants of the age are eager to attend, and lay out articles from all countries. The people of His Majesty's Harem come, and the women of other men are also invited, and buying and selling is quite general. His Majesty uses such days to select any articles which he wishes to buy, or to fix the prices of things, and thus add to his knowledge. The secrets of the empire, the character of the people, the good and bad qualities of each office and workshop, will then appear. His Majesty gives to such days the name of *Khushrūz*, or the joyful day, as they are a source of much enjoyment.[18]

In paintings one occasionally sees imperial womenfolk, either as proud mothers, formally posed with babe in arms in the harem compound, or surrounded by attendants, mothers-in-law, jealous would-be mothers, and girl musicians. More rarely, women are shown peeping out from windows or from behind curtains at their husbands' activities. Gossip and intrigue must have seethed in the ladies' quarters; but books such as *The History of Humāyūn* by Gul-Badan Begam ("Princess Rose Body") are scarcely more informative on this score than those by male authors.[19] Inasmuch as Akbar spent much time in the harem, we can assume that at least some of his three hundred wives were familiar not only with his statesmanly activities and personal life, but also with his music and art. The severely restricted ladies of the harem must have been among the keenest observers, and their opinions probably influenced the emperor's patronage. Conceivably, such delightful small manuscripts as Anvari's *Dīvān* were commissioned with some lady in mind, for Abu'l-Fazl tells us that part of the imperial library was kept in the harem.

Akbar's autocratic tendencies meshed well with the paternal attitude expected of him by most of his people, to whom he was the *Mai Bāp*, or "mother and father." Nevertheless, he seems to have been a difficult parent within his immediate family, particularly to his sons. In any society the lot of sons of eminent men is hard, but Akbar's sons must have felt overshadowed on a superhuman scale. The emperor's omnitalents, physical might, universal interests, and imperial sway left few, if any, areas in which a son could make his mark and thereby develop his own strength.

The birth of a male heir came late to Akbar, who eagerly sought one by his annual pilgrimages to Ajmer, to the tomb of Mu'inuddin, founder of the Chishti order. Although twin sons were born and died in 1564, the first male child to survive was Prince Salim, whose birth in 1569 was ascribed to the auspicious powers of the Chishtis. Sheikh Salim Chishti, who lived in Sikri, a village near the battlefield where Babur defeated Rana Sanga, assured Akbar that he would have three sons. When Akbar's first Hindu wife, the daughter of Raja Bihar Mal of Amber, became pregnant, he brought her to Sikri for the birth, which was gloriously celebrated. After a second son, Murad, was born there in 1570, also the year of the conquest of Gujarat, the village was renamed Fathabad, or "town of victory." In 1571 it became known as Fathpur-Sikri. For the next fifteen years, this red sandstone city was Akbar's burgeoning capital. Daniyal, the third son, was born in 1572. More admirable than Murad, who became known primarily for carousing and who died at twenty-nine, Daniyal was a sensitive and accomplished poet as well as an able general. Nevertheless, he died at thirty of alcoholism, despite his father's best efforts to deny him access to liquor, which was smuggled to him, often in matchlock barrels, by corrupt guards.

Prince Salim, who inherited the throne as Jahangir, or "World Seizer," was one of his gifted dynasty's more sensitive, creative, and beguiling emperors. But he was also highly complex, and he could be cruel and mercurial. Greatly outshone as a statesman and warrior by his father, he can be admired as a highly original and connoisseurly patron of painting and as the author of ramblingly delightful memoirs that are as fascinating for their trivia as for their candor.[20] For many years he was an outwardly obedient son; but he harbored jealousy and malice toward his father, and these eventually broke loose. In 1601 he rebelled, seizing Allahabad along with the revenues of Bihar. Although he set himself up as an independent king, he softened the blow to his father by honoring him as the "great king."

Akbar was deeply distressed, but he accepted Salim's government of Allahabad and in addition conferred Bengal and Orissa. In 1602, however, when Salim had the gall to strike gold and copper coins in his own name, the emperor lost patience and notified Abu'l-Fazl, then serving in the Deccan, who promised to defeat Salim and bring him bound before his father. Salim countered by sending Bir Singh of Orchha at the head of five hundred horsemen to ambush Abu'l-Fazl. Despite warnings, Abu'l-Fazl refused an adequate escort. At Sarai Barar, while preparing for the day's march, Abu'l-Fazl was attacked, speared, and decapitated. Akbar's closest friend's head was sent to Salim, who is said to have ordered it thrown into a privy. Despite this horrible test of fatherly devotion, Akbar again forgave Salim, and in 1603, when the prince suffered the loss of his first, greatly beloved wife, Akbar sent him a warm letter along with a robe of honor and his own turban, a symbolic reaffirmation of Salim's position as heir apparent.

In 1604, when Salim again showed signs of rebelliousness, Akbar reluctantly decided to bring him to heel — by military force, if necessary. But while the campaign was being readied, Akbar's mother, who doted on Salim, died. In her honor, military action was rejected in favor of diplomacy, and Salim was persuaded to come to Agra and submit to his father. The prince was received with cordial pomp, or so it seemed — but then his father's pent-up feelings erupted in fury. Akbar yanked Salim into a private chamber, slapped his face, and ranted at him. Salim was then confined in a bathroom, where he was watched over like a mental patient by a doctor and guards for twenty-four hours, a confinement made worse by the denial of opium, to which he was then addicted. But again Akbar's essential devotion won out; he himself brought his son the drug. The prince was soon pardoned and assigned quarters at Agra, where he remained until his father's death in 1605.

Akbar had many friends, some of whom were boon companions, people in whose company he delighted. Nine of them were known as his Nauratna, the "nine jewels" of the imperial inner circle. Of these, the closest to the emperor was Sheikh Abu'l-Fazl, son of Sheikh Mubarak and brother of the poet Faizi, who were also intimates of the emperor. Abu'l-Fazl first attracted Akbar's attention in 1574 as the author of a commentary on the Koran. Later he became the emperor's private secretary, an informal post that gave him more power than anyone else in the empire short of his master. Much of our information about Akbar's India is from Abu'l-Fazl's *Akbarnāma*, which probably was begun in the late 1580s. This extremely long, informative, but propagandistic history includes a final section called *A'īn-i Akbarī* ("The Mode of Governing"), in which everything from the imperial household, treasuries, gold and silver refining, the harem, encampment on journeys, ensigns of royalty, carpets and tents, the kitchen and its recipes, fruits, flavors, perfumes, elephants, horses, the army, hunting, to the library and the arts of writing and painting are discussed in lively detail. The *A'īn* was completed in 1596; the history itself was kept up to date virtually until the author's death in 1602, after which it was carried through the reign by 'Inayatullah Muhibb 'Ali.

Although we tend to imagine Abu'l-Fazl devotedly carrying out Akbar's instructions and jotting down his sayings, he was in fact a colorful and independent figure whose private opinions may not always have accorded with those of his emperor. Even as he abetted Akbar's eccentric religious programs, he is said to have been discovered by Prince Salim piously directing forty scribes as they copied out the Koran. Generously proportioned, Abu'l-Fazl was a noted gourmet who apparently consumed thirty pounds of food a day. He was also hospitable; according to a Mughal biographical dictionary, while he was in the Deccan toward the end of his life he maintained a large tent in which "every day one thousand plates of food were prepared and distributed among all the officers. Outside...cooked *kichiri* [rice and lentils] was distributed all day long to whoever wanted it – high or low."[21]

In the *Akbarnāma* Abu'l-Fazl offers appealing autobiographical insights:

> As fortune did not at first assist me, I almost became selfish and conceited, and resolved to tread the path of proud retirement. The...pupils I had gathered round me served but to increase my pedantry.... Pride of learning had made my brain drunk with the idea of seclusion. Happily,...when I passed the nights in lonely spots with true seekers after truth,...my eyes were opened and I saw the selfishness and covetousness of the so-called learned.... My mind had no rest, and my heart felt itself drawn to the sages of Mongolia, or to the hermits of Lebanon; I longed for interviews with the lamas of Tibet or with the padrīs of Portugal, and I would gladly sit with the priests of the Parsis and the learned of the Zendavesta.... My brother and other relatives then advised me to attend the court, hoping that I would find in the Emperor a leader to the sublime world of thought.... Happy, indeed, am I now that I have found in my sovereign a guide to the world of action and a comforter in lonely retirement.[22]

After Abu'l-Fazl was slain, Akbar was approached by his late friend's secretary bearing a blue kerchief, symbolic of death. For several days after receiving the terrible news, the emperor saw no one. Then he spoke: "If Salim wished to be emperor, he might have killed me and spared Abu'l-Fazl."[23]

Another of the "nine jewels" was Raja Birbal, who was born in 1528, as a poor Brahman with the name Mahesh Das. Fourteen years older than Akbar, he was sent to the imperial court by Raja Bhagwan Das early in the reign. A poet, storyteller, and wit, he was given the title of *kabi rai,* or poet laureate, by Akbar, who was charmed by his conversation. Akbar awarded him the fief of Kalanjar, in Bundelkhand, which was referred to by Badaoni, who detested Birbal, as "that dog's *jāgīr.*" To Akbar's deep grief, Birbal was killed in an Afghan ambush in 1586. The episode was noted gloatingly by Badaoni: "Bir Bar [Birbal], who had fled from fear of his life, was slain, and entered the row of the dogs in hell, and thus got something for the abominable deeds he had done during his lifetime."[24]

Raja Man Singh of Amber, also a "jewel," joined Akbar's court in 1562, at the time of the emperor's marriage to the eldest daughter of Raja Bihar Mal of Amber, who had adopted Man Singh. Two years later, Man Singh was given the first of many appointments by Akbar, who eventually honored him with the command of seven thousand horse, a position of extreme authority. Man Singh served at the siege of the Hara fort of Ranth-ambhor in 1569, as well as in many notable campaigns. It was he who probably saved Akbar's life when the intoxicated emperor attempted to outdo the Rajputs – prone to settling rivalries by running at the points of a double-ended spear – by hurling himself at his own sword. Man Singh knocked down the weapon, which cut Akbar's finger. Enraged, the emperor jumped on the Raja and began to throttle him. He was saved by another brave courtier, Sayyid Muzaffar, who twisted the bleeding imperial finger until the noble Rajput was released.

Although Man Singh was a proud Rajput, his proximity to the imperial throne offended the senior prince of Rajasthan, Rana Pratap Singh of Mewar, who refused either to eat with him or to receive him in person. When Akbar learned of this, he mounted a campaign against the Rana, who had so stubbornly held out against Mughal authority. A powerful army, led by Man Singh and the Muslim general Asaf Khan, was dispatched to Mewar. Even the extremely orthodox Muslim Badaoni participated, eager to vanquish a Hindu foe. During the heat of the battle, he and Asaf Khan, unable to differentiate between hostile and friendly Rajputs, cynically fired away at the mountain-like mass of men, certain of the rewards due those who fought the infidels.[25]

The Mewar campaign culminated in the siege of Haldighat, from which eight thousand of twenty-two thousand Mewar warriors survived the day. Rana Pratap escaped, however, despite his wounds, a circumstance for which Akbar blamed Man Singh, who may have held back his armies in loyalty to the premier Rajput. Man Singh earned his emperor's ire again on another occasion. In 1587, after he had been assigned the government of Bihar, Hajipur, and Patna, he was invited by Akbar to become one of the disciples of the Divine Faith. "I am a Hindu," was the reply. "But if you order me to become a Muslim I will do so. . . . I know not the existence of any other religion than these two." Akbar sent him to Bengal, where he held the office of governor during the rest of the reign. Man Singh died in the ninth regnal year of Jahangir. Sixty wives joined him on the funeral pyre in acts of *suttee.*

Raja Todar Mal, a Hindu of the clerical Kayastha caste, was born in Oudh to a family from the Punjab. Usually singled out as Akbar's most capable administrator as well as general, Todar Mal was valued for his intelligence and efficiency, not his charm. Abu'l-Fazl's accounts of him lack enthusiasm, and intolerant Badaoni disliked him almost as vehemently as he did Raja Birbal. Already in the imperial service by 1565, Todar Mal was entrusted with tax assessments in Gujarat in 1573-74, a task he carried out so energetically and intelligently that he became one of Akbar's most valued officers. In 1577-78 he led the imperial army against Sultan Muzaffar of Gujarat, a further success for which he was appointed *vazīr*. Although he began as a humble clerk, this "jewel" reached the position of *vakīl*, or prime minister, and in 1582-83 he was appointed *dīvān* (finance minister). In 1589, as a feeble old man, he applied for permission to retire to the holy city of Hardwar on the Ganges. At first Akbar agreed to the proposal, but he then recalled his valued officer with the order that "no worship of God was equal to taking care of the weak. It was therefore better that he should look after the affairs of the oppressed. He was obliged to return."[26] A few months later he died.

Akbar's serious enthusiasm for music was represented among the Nauratna by Miyan Tansen, a Hindu singer and instrumentalist who became a Muslim and was awarded the title *mirza*.[27] Trained by Adili, the last of the Sur kings, and at Gwalior, a music center patronized by Raja Man Singh Tomar (1486-1518), Tansen was sent for by Akbar from the court of Raja Ramchand of Bhatha, or Riwa, in 1562. Abu'l-Fazl wrote that "a singer like him has not been in India for the last thousand years." A friend of the great Hindi poet Sur Das, Tansen died in 1589 and was buried at Gwalior, where his tomb is a shrine frequently visited by musicians.

It was characteristic of Akbar's free-and-easy court style that most of his "nine jewels" served in many capacities. Hakim Humam, for instance, combined the talents of calligrapher, connoisseur of poetry, scientist, doctor, and diplomat. His official post, however, was as *mīr bakāwal*, or the "master of the kitchen." During his absences on official missions, Akbar often remarked: "Since Hakim Humam has gone, my food has not the same taste."[28]

Akbar's friends were as varied as his interests, which they reflected. When the emperor was on his deathbed, in October 1605, Father Jerome Xavier and some other Jesuits gravely approached the palace, to which they were admitted for what they supposed would be a morbid scene. But, as they neared Akbar's chamber, they realized that it was filled with courtiers and that the mood was one of "hilarum et laetum." They withdrew. A few days later, Akbar's condition had worsened. Although he could not speak, he directed Prince Salim to put on the imperial turban and Humayun's sword. Later, after Salim had left, Akbar is said to have died trying to pronounce the name of God.

Akbar's patronage of painting ranks with his other creative activities, and, like most of them, was a source of personal joy as well as an aspect of his statesmanly ambitions. As a boy in 1555, after the return of the Mughals to Delhi, he was guided in painting, according to Abu'l-Fazl, "by such fine and painstaking artists as Mir Sayyid-'Ali and 'Abdussamad," the remarkable royal Safavid artists recruited during Humayun's exile in Iran. Although Akbar's enthusiasm for painting was lifelong, Abu'l-Fazl's enlightening account of the emperor's involvement with it was written late in the sixteenth century:

> His Majesty, from his earliest youth has shown a great predilection for this art, and gives it every encouragement, as he looks upon it as a means, both of study and amusement. Hence the art flourishes, and many painters have obtained great reputation. The works of all painters are weekly laid before His Majesty by the *Dārōghas* [commandants of the ateliers] and the clerks; he then confers rewards according to excellence of workmanship, or increases the monthly salaries. Much progress was made in the commodities required by painters, and the correct prices of such articles were carefully ascertained. The mixture of colours has especially been improved. The pictures thus received a hitherto unknown finish. Most excellent painters are now to be found, and masterpieces, worthy of a Bihzad, may be placed at the side of the wonderful works of the European painters who have attained a world-wide fame. The minuteness in detail, the general finish, the boldness of execution, etc., now observed in pictures, are incomparable; even inanimate objects look as if they had life. More than a hundred painters have become famous masters of the art, whilst the number of those who approach perfection, or of those who are middling, is very large. This is especially true of the Hindus: their pictures surpass our conception of things. Few, indeed, in the whole world are found equal to them.

After briefly discussing four artists and citing thirteen others, the author continues:

> I have to notice that the observing of the figures of objects and the making of likenesses of them, which are often looked upon as an idle occupation, are, for a well regulated mind, a source of wisdom, and an antidote against the poison of ignorance. Bigoted followers of the letter of the law are hostile to the art of painting; but their eyes now see the truth. One day at a private party of friends, His Majesty, who had conferred on several the pleasure of drawing near to him, remarked: "There are many that hate painting; but such men I dislike. It appears to me as if a painter has a quite peculiar means of recognizing God; for a painter in sketching anything that has life, and in devising its limbs, one after another, must come to feel that he cannot bestow individuality upon his work, and is thus forced to think of God, the Giver of life, and will thus increase in knowledge."
>
> The number of master-pieces of painting increased with the encouragement given to the art. Persian books, both prose and poetry, were ornamented with pictures, and a very large number of paintings was thus collected. *The Story of Hamzah* [*Dāstān-i Amīr Ḥamza*, or *Ḥamzanāma*] was represented in twelve volumes, and clever painters made the most astonishing illustrations for no

less than one thousand and four hundred passages of the story. The Chinghiz-nama, the Zafarnama, this book, the Razmnama, the Ramayana, the Nal Daman, the Kalila Damnah, the 'Ayar Danish etc. were all illustrated. His Majesty himself sat for his likeness and also ordered to have the likenesses taken of all the grandees of the realm. An immense album was thus formed: those that have passed away have received a new life, and those who are still alive have immortality promised them.[29]

In describing one of the four artists, Khwaja ("master") 'Abdussamad, the biographer sheds further light on Akbar as a patron: "Though he had developed his art before joining the [Mughal] court, he was stirred to new heights by the alchemy of Akbar's vision, and he turned from outer to inner meaning. Under the tutelage of the Khwajeh, masterful students were produced."[30] Thus we learn that Akbar's charisma extended into the ateliers and enabled him to change 'Abdussamad's elegantly formal Safavid style into the more immediate, powerfully naturalistic – at times super-naturalistic – idiom preferred by the emperor.

Akbar's thoughts on Safavid painting can be surmised by a passage in the *Akbarnāma*, although the words originally described writing rather than painting: "Most old authors, who string out their words . . . and display a worn out embroidery give all their attention to the ornamentation of words, and regard matter as subservient to them, and so exert themselves in a reverse direction. They consider cadence and decorative style as the constituents of eloquence and think that prose should be tricked out like the words of poets."[31]

Greatly to Akbar's taste was the work of the Hindu Daswanth (or Dasawanta), another of the four painters singled out by Abu'l-Fazl. He was "the son of a palkee [palanquin]-bearer. He devoted his whole life to the art, and used, from love of his profession, to draw and paint figures even on walls. One day the eye of His Majesty fell on him; his talent was discovered, and he himself handed over to the Khwajeh. In a short time he surpassed all painters, and became the first master of the age. Unfortunately, the light of his talents was dimmed by the shadow of madness; he committed suicide. He has left many masterpieces."[32]

A great school of painting like Akbar's was not only enormously costly to maintain, but also required the degree of continuing devotion shown by many of his dynasty, who rank among the foremost royal patrons of all time. Unlike more fastidious enthusiasts of painting, such as Shah Tahmasp or Emperor Jahangir, both of whom were typical of a second generation, Akbar, the refounder of the Mughal school as well as of the empire, appreciated and encouraged a wide spectrum of talent instead of cultivating a small cadre of great artists. Although, as Abu'l-Fazl wrote, he employed more than a hundred major masters, there were many others in his ateliers whose work could not have passed muster under Jahangir. Indeed, on coming to the throne, Jahangir released many of his father's painters, most of whom found work in the bazaars of Agra or moved to Rajput courts.

One senses that Akbar's artists were more varied in every way than those of his son. Just as the empire expanded through Akbar's efforts, so did the painting workshops. Although some artists were inherited from Humayun, many more were recruited from Indian courts forced into the Mughal sway or attracted by the emperor's reputation as a stimulating and secure patron. With incredible speed, the earlier styles of painters from Gujarat, Varanasi, and Bengal gave way to the new Mughal synthesis under the direction of such masters as Mir Sayyid-'Ali and 'Abdussamad, usually under the emperor's own watchful eye. Most of these recruits must have been from relatively simple backgrounds, for traditional Indian artists did not rank high on the social scale. Akbar's refreshing obliviousness to accepted conventions must have been encouraging to these remarkable but unworldly people and doubtless spurred them on to new heights. Presumably the emperor's respect for ability over background was embraced by the Safavid masters, particularly by 'Abdussamad, a wellborn man of Shiraz, who served as a moderately high government official as well as artist in residence in the painting studios. We suspect that Mir Sayyid-'Ali's comparatively ingrown and hypersensitive personality, which led to his departure for Mecca in 1570 following some sort of emotional trouble, made him a less successful teacher.[33] But these two Iranians, along with a few others, must have been among the few courtier-artists. Most of the official painters were less august. According to the *A'īn*, "Many *Manṣabdārs* [officers], *Aḥādīs* [enlisted men], and other soldiers hold appointments in the [painting] department. The pay of foot soldiers varies from 1,200 to 600 dams."[34] This modest pay scale was surely made more tolerable by bonuses for superior achievement in the ateliers.

Artists were part of Akbar's entourage, accompanying him on hunts and campaigns. Like our photographers, they were on-the-scene reporters of all consequential missions and events. Much of their time must have been spent sketching from life, an enlivening occupation that lends immediacy to their finished work. Such drawings of the Akbar period, however, are scarce, perhaps because they were kept and referred to by the artists rather than mounted, as became the custom later, in illuminated borders for the royal albums.

FIGURE 3. Study of an artist at work. From an album of Emperor
Jahangir. Berlin State Library, Orientabteilung. MS 117, fol. 21a.

In Mughal India pictures were both painted and enjoyed on ground level, usually while the artist or viewer was seated on a carpet or mat. Except for the monumental pictures from the *Dāstān-i Amīr Ḥamza*, manuscripts and albums of large size were propped up on book stands or tabourets. More intimately scaled manuscripts, like the *Dīvān* of Anvari, were held in the hand, to better enjoy the feel of the binding, hear the rustle of paper, and relish the fineness of the illustrations. Artists, as can be seen in a miniature of about 1590 from one of Jahangir's albums, sat as they drew or painted, with one knee raised to support a drawing board to which the picture was fastened (Figure 3). Often they began miniatures by tracing drawings from nature onto a fresh piece of paper or pasteboard, made by gluing together layers of paper. Tracing, or pouncing, was accomplished by placing a piece of transparent gazelle skin over the picture to be copied and outlining the subject with a reed pen or brush. The skin was then pricked along the outlines and placed on top of the picture in progress. Black pigment was then rubbed through the holes, leaving a fuzzy silhouette. This indefinite outline was later sharpened with the point of a brush dipped into gray, black, or occasionally dark red watercolor. Errors were corrected by covering them with opaque white pigment and redrawing. Colors, kept in clamshells, were brushed on layer by layer, each of which was burnished by being placed upside down on a smooth surface, then gently rubbed with a polished agate or crystal. The binding medium, mixed with water from a handy little bowl, was probably glue or gum arabic, but this is the least-known aspect of an exceedingly subtle technique. As can be seen in the portrait of an artist at work, spectacles were available.

Occasionally painters worked on walls, cotton, or silk rather than paper, which was so excellently made from cloth fibers that, barring accidental damage, it survives unscathed. Brushes were made from bird quills, into which baby squirrels' or kittens' hairs were tied. All such "trade secrets" were learned by apprentices, probably as young children.

Pigments varied greatly in material, permanence, and resistance to fading. Some coloring agents, such as saffron, were extremely fugitive; others, including the metals and most minerals, such as lapis lazuli and malachite, resisted the effects of light. Gold, silver, and copper were the primary metallic pigments, which were first pounded into thin foil between layers of leather, then ground up in a mortar, using salt as an abrasive. This was washed out, leaving the powdered metal, which was brushed on in a binding medium. In spite of the certainty of tarnishing, silver was used for such passages as water, usually with the addition of fine white or black brush drawing to suggest ripples. Gold was applied either pure or with the admixture of silver to make it lighter, or copper for a warmer tone. Highlights could be created by burnishing small areas or by stippling the surface with a steel needle to add glitter. Sometimes whites were built up in tooled relief patterns before being painted with gold.

Other pigments were made from earth and assorted dyes of vegetal, animal, and insect origin. So-called Indian yellow was the result of a complex process involving camel urine; cochineal required crushing parts of special beetles.

Mughal artists can be divided into two categories: masters, also known as designers or outliners, and colorists, perhaps "pigmenters," who were apprentices or assistants – not deemed worthy of working alone. Wondrous projects like the *Hamzanāma* were carefully planned by the emperor in conjunction with the director, in this case first Mir Sayyid-'Ali followed by 'Abdussamad. The director or another leading master outlined ("designed") each composition, after which a lesser painter applied the colors. Presumably the master closely supervised each stage of the picture's progress and often painted areas of particular interest to him. When at Fathpur-Sikri, Akbar would have kept a keen eye on the enterprise.

Miniatures in most important manuscripts of the Akbar period are inscribed with the artists' names in the lower margin, written by the clerks of the workshop. *Adham Khan Being Thrown from the Wall at Agra* (Figure 1) bears the name of the master artist Miskin as "outliner" and as "painter of special portraits." Shankar is given as "painter." Occasionally a third or fourth artist contributed other special passages to a miniature. Such division of labor, which followed Safavid practice, was usual for manuscripts like the *Hamzanāma*, historical volumes, or translations of Hindu epics, all of which required many important illustrations. At times, however, these official productions include a few pictures carried out by a single master.

Akbar's paintings provide sensitive indications of his developing personality. The illustrations for the *Hamzanāma*, his early and most grandiose project, reflect the immensity of the emperor's youthful exuberance. Far larger than most other Akbar-period pictures – measuring approximately two and a half feet by two feet – they were painted like Tibetan *tankas* on cotton backed by paper, upon which the Persian text was written in elegant but forceful *nasta'līq* script. The text was intended to be read aloud from the back while the illustrations were held up to an audience, a practice still current in Indian villages and one that must have been familiar to Raja Birbal, who began life as a *bādfarosh*, or bard. Akbar's enthusiasm for these vivid stories is underscored by a passage in the *Akbarnāma* stating that in 1564 during a hunting expedition "for the sake of delight and pleasure he listened for some time to Darbar Khan's recital of the story of Amir Hamza."[35] Those legendary picaresque tales were spun around the distinguished bearded figure of Amir Hamza, whose character was based upon the mistaken unification of two personages of the same name, an uncle of the prophet and a popular Iranian hero from Sistan. The fantastic stories perfectly suited the rough-and-tumble atmosphere of the dynamic young emperor's court from about 1566 until 1580, when the vast project was the major effort of the ateliers.[36]

According to Badaoni, the *Hamzanāma* was completed over a period of fifteen years in sixteen illustrated volumes, each individually boxed, each differing slightly. Abu'l-Fazl wrote that the epic was done in twelve volumes with fourteen hundred illustrations, of which about ten percent have survived – many of them damaged and retouched.[37] They were the principal training ground for Akbar's frantically productive corps of artists. *A Quarrel Among Hamza's Friends* (Figure 4) exemplifies the *Hamzanāma's* larger-than-life quality with its kaleidoscopic arabesques, violent richness, and aggressive cast of grinning, snarling, and hirsute zanies, seemingly caged by the posts and fences of a throne-pavilion. Like most of the figures in the series, these seem wildly dramatized and caricaturish, either grossly obese, muscle-bound, or lean as praying mantises. Their masklike grotesquerie, abnormal sizes, and empathic gesticulations, however, are so convincing that they sweep us into the swarming circus of Akbar's Fathpur-Sikri.

The *Hamzanāma's* stacatto areas of color and surging, implosive forms parallel the attraction of Akbar's formative empire, which tugged lands, riches, and people to it, as though by supernatural force. This energetic phase ended, with the *Hamza* project, in about 1580, by which time Akbar had experienced his fulfilling vision and the state had attained stability. Nevertheless, perpetually ambitious Akbar was dissatisfied, spiritually and temporally. Always a seeker, he invited the first mission of Jesuit priests from Goa to Fathpur-Sikri in 1578. Two years later they arrived, with high but futile hopes of converting Akbar, and, with him, all of Mughal India. Their voices joined the others in the *'ibādat-khāna* (hall of worship). Although the emperor got on well with Father Aquaviva, he eventually lost interest in theological argumentation, so much of which

must have descended to wrangling and scholasticism. The debates were ended in the summer of 1582, the year of the Divine Faith and the occasion of a burst dam at Fathpur-Sikri.

During the years of the *Hamza* project, other illustrated manuscripts and albums were also being painted in the royal workshops. Several of these have survived, showing the development of the Mughal style and the emperor's evolving tastes, which progressed from dynamic, earthy simplicity toward classical refinements. The earliest manuscript is a fulsomely illustrated copy of Ziya'uddin Nakhshabi's *Ṭūṭīnāma* ("Tales of a Parrot"),[38] most of which is in the Cleveland Museum of Art. Datable to the early 1560s, the book, with its 218 known miniatures, is a product of the earliest phase of Akbar's ateliers. The subjects illustrate the emperor's youthful zest for entertaining fables, and many of the illustrations reveal in varying degrees the artists' styles prior to their recruitment by the Mughal atelier – styles associated with pre-Mughal Muslim and Hindu traditions. Others of its pictures, such as those ascribed to the famed painters Basawan and Daswanth, show that these progressive artists had already become adherents of the new Mughal synthesis.

Although many of the *Ṭūṭīnāma's* small miniatures were influenced by the *Hamzanāma*, none can be closely linked to that project's directors. One of the outstanding pictures, *The Hunter Sells the Mother Parrot to the King of Kamro* (Figure 5), is already fully attributable on stylistic grounds to Basawan, whose name is inscribed on it. Even at this formative stage of Akbari painting, Basawan's psychologically observed figures, masterful and painterly brushwork, and sculpturesque view of form reveal him as one of the atelier's avant-garde. By the early 1560s European prints, with their rounded modeling, suggestions of deep space, and portraiture, may have reached Akbar and his artists. Basawan's "European" qualities, nevertheless, seem to have been fundamental characteristics of his artistic personality, which was little more than catalyzed by seeing Western solutions to common visual problems.

The *Ṭūṭīnāma's* uneven quality, its pre-Mughal as well as fully synthesized styles of painting, and its lack of fineness gave way to the more resolved qualities of a somewhat larger manuscript dated 1568, Amir Khusrau of Delhi's *'Ashiqa* ("Love Epic").[39] Its two miniatures are painted in a more miniaturistic adaptation of the fully evolved *Hamza* idiom. Finer still are most of the twenty-seven or so pictures for a copy of Husain Va'iz-i

FIGURE 4. A Quarrel Among Hamza's Friends. From the *Hamzanāma*, The Metropolitan Museum of Art, New York. Rogers Fund, 1918: 18.44.2.

45

Kashifi's *Anvār-i Suhailī* ("The Lights of Canopus"), dated 1570.[40] Many of these miniatures bring to mind royal Safavid work in the minutia of their execution, but the palette and rhythms are lower-keyed equivalents of the *Ḥamza* paintings, lacking their gusto. Perhaps they represent the standard of finish aspired to by the ex-Safavid masters. One suspects that this manuscript was overly polished to suit the still-young emperor's penchant for liveliness.

More to his taste, we believe, was a fascinating manuscript of Abu Tahir Tarasusi's *Dārābnāma* ("The Story of Darab"). It appears to have been illustrated in about 1585 and documents Akbar's state of mind at the time he moved from Fathpur-Sikri to Lahore.[41]

In 1580 Akbar's brother Muhammad Hakim of Kabul had brazenly sent raiding parties into the Punjab, and in the following year he unwisely went there himself. The distressed emperor countered the attack by leading a force to Kabul, easily curbing the mirza's rambunctiousness. Proud of his accomplishment, which had tested the might of his empire, Akbar sent an abortive mission to Portugal, which he imagined – not unreasonably – to be the leading European nation. The emissaries were to have proclaimed Akbar's rule and proposed a joint venture against Ottoman Turkey. No scheme was too imaginative or grandiose! At the same time, the emperor was busily modifying the revenue system and building a new fort at Allahabad.

But Akbar always wanted more. After Prince Salim's marriage in 1584 at Fathpur-Sikri, the emperor moved the capital northwestward to Lahore, a strategic location in case of threats from the Uzbeks, who were now aggressively led by 'Abdullah Khan. Perhaps, too, the move was prompted by boredom with the completed Fathpur-Sikri, which Akbar was not to see again for thirteen years. Lahore, the new capital, offered fresh challenges – new fortifications, gardens, and palaces. It was also ideally situated as a base of operations from which to reconnoiter new territories. The prospect of annexing Kashmir – later referred to by Akbar as "my garden" – was secondary only to capturing the hills of Badakhshan, noted for their jewels, and retaking the ancestral realms of Turan (Transoxiana), from which the emperor's grandfather had been driven earlier in the century.

Many of the *Dārābnāma*'s 157 miniatures bear in their lower margins attributions to court painters. These include several new artists, recently hired at Lahore, with names such as Ibrahim Lahori and Kalu Lahori, whose somewhat crude, angular manner, with attenuated figures, represents the bazaar-level recollections of a now little-known sultanate style.[42]

46

روز دیگر طوطی معلاج رای مشغول شد و خدمت پسندیده کرد و ذکر چنانکه
رای رای و اعتماد تمام شد و اعتقاد کلی کشت و لاز و دویة و اشربه اوننی زحمت
رای یوف یکروز طوطی آغاز کرد رای ای رای چون بواسطه من ننی زحمت نوزائد
شد نو مراد در زحمت تمام بیند و چون گناهکاران در زندان قفص مدار
پر و بال شکسته من از جهن قفص بیرون آور و بطرف صحرا سرای خود بدار به

FIGURE 5. The Hunter Sells the Mother Parrot to the King of Kamro. From the
Ṭūṭīnāma, Cleveland Museum of Art. Gift of Mrs. A. Dean Perry. 62.279/36b.

(Lahore had been a major center of Muslim culture in India since the eleventh century, when it was the capital of the Ghaznavid dynasty.) The *Dārābnāma* also contains outstanding miniatures by Akbar's familiar masters, such as Kesu, Khem Karan, Miskin, and Basawan,[43] all of whom were now working in more developed and accomplished versions of their earlier styles. Daswanth, alas, had committed suicide in 1584 and is not represented.

In comparison to the *Ḥamzanāma* pictures, those for the *Dārābnāma* are considerably calmer, although the tales they illustrate are equally fantastic. One can imagine the emperor's amusement upon seeing such paintings as one of an astonished horseman being swallowed up, steed and all, by a hulking dragon.[44] He must have been equally intrigued by two depictions of nude bodies, never before represented so accurately in Islamic art. A particularly appealing and characteristic illustration, *'Abkarhud Being Acclaimed King by His Followers* (Figure 6), ascribed to Madhu Khurd, reveals many of the new directions being explored by Akbar's eager artists. In it, the colors and forms are more restrained and true to life than those in the *Ḥamzanāma;* the rhythms and patterns are almost somber in comparison, and space is described with credibly airy softness. Although the brushwork remains vitally fresh, a remarkable new characteristic is evident, one well suited to the emperor's period of maturity: true portraiture. Previously, as in the *Ḥamzanāma* illustrations (see Figure 4), personages, however effectively dramatized, conformed to types rather than to individuals. Now, one senses actual people, accurately depicted down to the last expressively raised eyebrow, aquiline nose, or ample belly. Fortunately, it is possible to recognize the gathering of worthy gentlemen shown here, for their turbans and costumes are of the sort worn at the sultanate of Ahmadnagar in the Deccan. One of the figures, a stocky fellow standing before the throne, can be identified as Burhan Nizam Shah II of Ahmadnagar (r. 1591-95), who is known to have received sanctuary prior to his accession at Lahore in 1585. His entourage was received at court by Akbar on March 21 of that year, on the occasion of the Nauroz festival.[45] A well-known portrait of this sultan in the Bibliothèque Nationale, Paris, shows him five or six years later.[46] The similarity to the *Dārābnāma* supports the present dating of the manuscript, which may have been started en route to the new capital and yields evidence of the artist's mastery of individual characterization, encouraged by his patron, whose view of portraiture is known through Abu'l-Fazl.

Like many active men, Akbar was not overly fond of classical poetry, at any rate, not until middle age. If the fervid young Akbar was more

FIGURE 6. 'Abkarhud Being Acclaimed King by His Followers. From the British Library, London. MS Or. 4615, fol. 74a.

49

interested in short, outlandishly imaginative tales like those of the *Ham-zanāma, Ṭūṭīnāma,* and *Dārābnāma,* his literary appetites seem to have favored subtler fare later on. The *Aīn* tells us that the poetry of Anvari was one of the books "continually read out to His Majesty."[47] Possibly the Fogg manuscript is the very copy to which Abu'l-Fazl referred, for it is a notably imperial manuscript, clearly the work of one of his best calligraphers, made on exceptionally fine marbleized paper and illustrated by the most admired court painters.

The extreme fineness, intimately small scale, and overall sumptuousness of this fourth earliest dated Mughal manuscript evoke a new mood in the dynasty's arts of the book.[48] Its delicate folios of calligraphy and gently romantic miniatures are far removed from the surging boldness of the giant *Hamza* project or even the subtler passages of the *Dārābnāma.* Why? No single explanation is adequate. Perhaps the tiny format required unprecedentedly fine workmanship, of which the now-well-established ateliers were capable. Basawan and his colleagues, it seems, were glorying in their achievements. A decade or so later, Abu'l-Fazl in the *Aīn* boasted of their pictures' "minuteness in detail . . . [and] general finish." But he also hailed their "boldness of execution,"[49] a quality still pronounced in this *Dīvān* and well worth the effort required to discern it. For the illustrators not only worked with the care and precision of jewelers; they also painted dashingly, with infinitely small yet sweeping brushstrokes. Abundant power lies beneath the nuances.

A glance at the chronology of Akbar's life shows that 1588 was one of his most leisurely years, which may also account for the *Dīvān*'s subtleties and sense of tranquillity. Such work required time, for both the artists and patron. Both, in these pictures, lingered over the myriad figures, each scarcely larger than an eyelash, yet imbued with living presence. Settings, too, were planned with eager care, as though the audience halls, bedchambers, and courtyards recalled past pleasures. Most of all, landscapes, such as the one in *The Poet's Journey* (Plate 5), haunt one with their credible poetry. Here, perhaps for the first time in Mughal painting, the artist has painted air, earth, vegetation, people, and animals with convincing spatial conviction. Through him we sense a pleasantly moist late afternoon, and, with the poet, we are urged to travel into the "globe of dust."

A further reason for the unprecedented delicacy and naturalism of the *Dīvān* might be the presence at Lahore of Prince Salim, who was the most enthusiastic and discerning lover of fine painting in the dynasty's long history. He remained at his father's court for thirteen years after his marriage at Fathpur-Sikri in 1584, when he was fifteen. But, in 1591, according to Badaoni, Akbar "suffered from stomach-ache and colic ... [and] ... in this unconscious state ... uttered some words which rose from suspicion of his eldest son, and accused him of giving him poison."[50] Until this falling out, Salim must have had access to the imperial painting studios, where his devotion to art would have been influential. Very likely father and son discussed painting often during these years.

Nineteen in the year of the *Dīvān*'s creation, Salim must have already been cultivating his appreciation of painting, presumably by frequent and lengthy visits to his father's atelier. Later, in his memoirs, he was to make the famous boast that

> my liking for painting and my practice in judging it have arrived at such a point that when any work is brought before me, either of deceased artists or those of the present day, without the names being told me, I say on the spur of the moment that it is the work of such and such a man. And if there be a picture containing many portraits, and each face be the work of a different master, I can discover which face is the work of each of them. If any other person has put in the eye and eyebrow of a face, I can perceive whose work the original face is, and who has painted the eye and eyebrow.[51]

Although formality was gaining at the Mughal court, in direct ratio to the increased restraint evident in painting, Salim's involvement with the court painters must have been intense and extremely educational. Surely he looked over Basawan's shoulder as the aging master painted *Anvari Entertains in a Summer House* (Plate 2), learning the secrets of brushwork and offering princely encouragement. Manohar, Basawan's son, was approximately the same age as Salim, and it is hardly coincidental that he painted several outstanding portraits of the prince.[52] One suspects that young Manohar painted *A Magnanimous Vizier* (Plate 3) and that its particularly believable characterizations were guided by the artistic prince. Gestures – including such personal ones as oddly jutting necks – brushwork, landscape, and facial types all look ahead to a miniature of about 1595 ascribed to Manohar from a scattered copy of Sa'di's *Gulistān* (Figure 7). This "fish story," concerning an ill-fated netman's struggle against one that got away, is fully representative of several magnificently finished manuscripts illustrated in the 1590s by Akbar's greatest masters, a group that leads directly to still more progressive ones made for Salim when he again had access to the imperial workshop after his enthronement as Emperor Jahangir. As a series, these are the most restrained and classically spirited manuscripts of Akbar's reign. Stylistically, they stem from the little Fogg *Dīvān*, which links them to Akbar's earlier, less tame projects, such as the *Ḥamzanāma* and *Dārābnāma*, of which it retains

افتاده بود تو انستی نگاه داشت گفتای اندر چه توان کرد هر روزی

بنو دوما سی از روزی چند باقی بو د مثل است که

هنر ور

FIGURE 7. A Huge Fish Netted. From a *Gulistān* of Sa'di, Cincinnati Art Museum. Gift of John J. Emery. 1950.284.

lively resonances. We believe that this magisterial series represents the combined efforts of the empire's most talented artists, fostered by both Akbar and Prince Salim during their years together at Lahore and Agra, where the court moved in 1598. Both men were devotees of painting, which may have been the sole activity in which their conflicting ways – Akbar's outgoing, purposeful dynamism and Salim's deeply peculiar perfectionism – could meet. When, in his memoirs, the son, usually so ambiguous toward his father, wrote of him with profound appreciation, he may have been warmed by thoughts of the creative years of their joint patronage:

> In his actions and movements he was not like the people of the world, and the glory of God manifested itself in him. . . . Notwithstanding his kingship, his fighting elephants and Arab horses, he never by a hair's breadth placed his foot beyond the base of humility before the throne of God, but considered himself the lowest of created beings, and never for one moment forgot God.[53]

NOTES

1. The Anvari *Dīvān* of Akbar is in the collection of the Fogg Art Museum, Harvard University (Gift of John Goelet, 1960.117.15). It was formerly in the collection of C. W. Dyson Perrins, who acquired it from Bernard Quaritch, London, in 1908. See Sotheby & Co., *The Dyson Perrins Collection*, pt. 2 (December 1, 1959), lot 93.

2. Jahangir, *The Tūzuk-i Jahāngīrī; or Memoirs of Jahāngīr*, trans. Alexander Rogers, ed. Henry Beveridge (London, 1909-14), 1: 33-34.

3. Babur, *The Memoirs of Bābur*, trans. Annette S. Beveridge (London, 1922), fasc. 3: 518.

4. Elizabeth A. Moynihan, *Paradise as a Garden in Persia and Mughal India* (New York, 1979), 96-109.

5. For discussions of these artists, see Martin Bernard Dickson and Stuart Cary Welch, *The Houghton Shahnameh* (Cambridge, Mass., 1981), 1: 178-200.

6. Dr. Ellen Smart has suggested that Akbar might have suffered from dyslexia.

7. Abu'l-Fazl, *The Akbarnāma*, trans. H. Beveridge (Calcutta, 1912), 2: 219.

8. This episode was immortalized in a double-page miniature now in the Victoria and Albert Museum, London. For a color reproduction, see Stuart Cary Welch, *Imperial Mughal Painting* (New York, 1978), pls. 12, 13.

9. Al-Badaoni [Abdul Qadir Bin Maluk Shah], *Muntakhab-ut-Tawārīkh*, trans. W. H. Lowe (Calcutta, 1884), 2: 203.

10. Al-Badaoni, *Muntakhab-ut-Tawārīkh*, 2: 335.

11. For a substantial pioneer discussion of this sort of experience, see Richard Maurice Bucke, *Cosmic Consciousness* (New York, 1901).

12. Abu'l-Fazl, *The Akbarnāma*, 3: 346-47.

13. Al-Badaoni, *Muntakhab-ut-Tawārīkh*, 2: 261.

14. Abu'l-Fazl, *The Akbarnāma*, 3: 354-55.

15. According to Islamic law, Hindus and Parsis were not "people of the book," but in practice the Mughals accepted them as such, along with Christians.

16. For illustrations of the Jaipur *Razm-nāma*, see Thomas H. Hendley, *Memorials of the Jeypore Exhibition 1883* (London, 1883), vol. 4. The *Rāmāyana* has not been published.

17. For the *Harivamsá*, see Robert Skelton, "Mughal Painting from the Harivamsá," in *Victoria and Albert Museum Yearbook, Number 2* (London, 1969), 41-54. See also Francis G. Hutchins, *Young Krishna* (West Franklin, N.H., 1980).

18. Abu'l-Fazl, *A'īn-i Akbarī*, trans. H. Blochmann (Calcutta, 1873), 1: 276-77.

19. Begam Gul-Badan (Princess Rose Body), *The History of Humāyūn*, trans. Annette S. Beveridge (London, 1902).

20. *The Tūzuk-i Jahāngīrī*, written between 1605 and 1623.

21. Samsam-ud-Daula (Shah Nawaz Khan) and 'Abdul Hayy, *The Maāthir-ul-Umarā*, trans. H. Beveridge and Beni Prashad (Calcutta, 1911-52), 2: 954.

22. Abu'l-Fazl, *The Akbarnāma*, 3: 116-17.

23. Abu'l-Fazl, *A'īn-i Akbarī*, xxvii.

24. Al-Badaoni, *Muntakhab-ut-Tawārīkh*, 2: 361.

25. Al-Badaoni, *Muntakhab-ut-Tawārīkh*, 2: 237.

26. Samsam-ud-Daula and 'Abdul Hayy, *The Maāthir-ul-Umarā*, 2: 954.

27. Although *mirza* often referred to royal princes, it was also a title applied to Turkish-Persian aristocracy.

28. Samsam-ud-Daula and 'Abdul Hayy, *The Maāthir-ul-Umarā*, 1: 607.

29. Abu'l-Fazl, *A'īn-i Akbarī*, 1: 107-9.

30. Dickson and Welch, *The Houghton Shahnameh*, 1: 195.

31. Abu'l-Fazl, *The Akbarnāma*, 2: 553.

32. Abu'l-Fazl, *A'īn-i Akbarī*, 1: 108.

33. Dickson and Welch, *The Houghton Shahnameh*, 1: 195.

34. William Irvine, *The Army of the Indian Moghuls* (London, 1903), 6.

35. Abu'l-Fazl, *The Akbarnāma*, 2: 343-44.

36. Dickson and Welch, *The Houghton Shahnameh*, 1: 178-200; also Pramod Chandra, *The Tuti-Nāma of the Cleveland Museum of Art*, with facsimile plates of the manuscript (Graz, 1976).

37. For illustrations, see Heinrich Glück, *Die indischen Miniaturen des Haemzae-romanes . . .* (Zurich, 1925); Gerhart Egger, ed., *Hamza-nāma* (Graz, 1974).

38. Chandra, *The Tuti-Nāma*, with its accompanying volume of facsimile plates of the manuscript, as well as the volume of translations (Muhammad A. Simsar, *The Cleveland Museum of Art's Tuti-Nāma/Tales of a Parrot* [Graz, 1978]).

39. In the National Museum of India, New Delhi; see Chandra, *The Tuti-Nāma*, pls. 35, 36.

40. In the Library, School of Oriental and African Studies, London; see Basil Gray, "Painting," in *Art of India and Pakistan, a Commemorative Catalogue of the Exhibition Held at the Royal Academy of Arts, London, 1947-8* (London, 1950), no. 636, col. pl. F, pl. 119. See also Chandra, *The Tuti-Nāma*, pls. 39-42.

41. British Library, London, MS Or. 4615. Norah M. Titley, *Miniatures from Persian Manuscripts* (London, 1977), 8-11. See also Welch, *Imperial Mughal Painting*, col. pls. 5, 6.

42. Stuart Cary Welch, *A Flower from Every Meadow* (New York, 1973), 86-87, no. 51, with illustration.

43. Welch, *Imperial Mughal Painting*, col. pl. 6.

44. Welch, *Imperial Mughal Painting*, col. pl. 5.

45. Radhey Shyam, *The Kingdom of Ahmadnagar* (Delhi, 1966), 179.

46. For a color plate of the portrait, see Douglas Barrett, *Painting of the Deccan, XVI-XVII Century* (London, 1958), pl. 5.

47. Abu'l-Fazl, *A'īn-i Akbarī*, 1: 109.

48. The three earlier manuscripts are the *'Āshiqa* of 1568, in the National Museum of India (see Chandra, *The Ṭuṭi-Nāma*, pls. 35, 36); the *Anvār-i Suhailī* of 1570, in the School of Oriental and African Studies, London (see Basil Gray, "Painting," in *Art of India and Pakistan*, no. 636; pl. 119); and a copy of Sa'di's *Gulistān*, copied at Fathpur-Sikri in 1581, now in the Royal Asiatic Society, London, for which, see Gray, "Painting," no. 642; pl.

121. This manuscript contains a very useful self-portrait by Manohar, which shows the artist seated facing a scribe. The latter portrait would seem to have been improved by the boy artist's father, Basawan.

49. Abu'l-Fazl, *A'īn-i Akbarī*, 1: 107.

50. Al-Badaoni, *Muntakhab-ut-Tawārīkh*, 2: 390.

51. Jahangir, *The Tūzuk-i Jahāngīrī*, 2: 20-21.

52. See especially A. A. Ivanov, T. V. Grek, and O. F. Akimushkin, *Al'bom indiyskikh i persiskikh miniatyur XVI-XVIII vv.* (The Album of Indian and Persian Miniatures of the 16th-18th Centuries) (Moscow, 1962), pl. 17, an extraordinary enthroned portrait, possibly done prior to 1605. Also see Laurence Binyon and Thomas Arnold, *Court Painters of the Grand Moguls* (Oxford, 1921), pl. 1, in color.

53. Jahangir, *The Tūzuk-i Jahāngīrī*, 1: 34-37.

ANVARI
AND HIS POETRY

The sphere poetic hath its prophets three
(Although "There is no Prophet after me!")
Firdausi in the epic; in the ode
Sa'di; and in qaṣīda *Anvari.* [1]

THIS VERSE was written by the fifteenth-century Persian poet Jami to assert the brilliance of Anvari, in "the light of whose mind the world of virtues became illuminated."[2]

Auhaduddin Anvari is the most celebrated panegyrist of his time – the twelfth century – but "it is difficult for a European student of Persian . . . to think of Anvari as the equal of Firdausi and Sa'di." Thus wrote E. G. Browne, to whom we owe the most extensive and perceptive account in English of Anvari's life and art.[3]

Shortly before Browne made his study, another historian of Persian literature, Hermann Ethé, praised Anvari:

High above all previously mentioned panegyrists of Sanjar stands this prince's favorite, Auhaduddin 'Ali Anvari, who is still celebrated by the critics as the greatest Persian writer of *qaṣīda*. If splendor and grandeur of language, an inexhaustible wealth of poetical metaphors, and a truly perfect gift of witty flattery entitle one to bear this honorific designation [*malik ash-shu'arā*, "king of poets"], then Anvari certainly deserves it; with him, panegyrics reached their zenith.[4]

Although Reuben Levy states that Anvari's *qaṣīdas* "make dull and difficult reading even to a Persian,"[5] the latest historian of Persian literature, Jan Rypka, sees Anvari as "probably one of the most brilliant figures in Persian literature" and points especially to the "exceedingly powerful scholarly element in his verse," quoting with approval Jami's statement that Anvari's *qaṣīdas* constitute "almost a miracle." Rypka speaks further of the poet's "inimitable facility" and perceives Anvari's biting sarcasm as well as his subtle humor.[6] For, as Anvari himself states in a verse, serious matters without a shade of levity are boring.[7] (To be honest, Anvari's humor often deteriorates into obscenity, which was not unusual among medieval Persian poets.)

Rypka's positive evaluation is taken up by Alessandro Bausani, who also quotes Jami's quatrain in which Anvari is ranked with Firdausi and Sa'di and calls him "truly the Sa'di of panegyrics," praising his fluent, natural style.[8] This contradicts Rypka's statement and the consensus of most readers that Anvari's *qaṣīdas* are barely comprehensible without a learned commentary.[9]

The Persian sources do not give many details of Anvari's life, but deal, as always, in generalities. According to the latest edition of the voluminous *Dīvān,* edited by Mudarris Razavi, Auhaduddin Anvari was born to a wealthy family in Abivard in northeastern Iran in about 1110. He was given a traditional education; in addition, he studied astrology, music, geometry, metaphysics, and other useful things. Persian scholars attribute a copy of the *Dīvān* of the Tabrizi poet Qatran, dated 529 A.H./A.D. 1135, to Anvari as calligrapher.[10] It is written in a rather ugly hand and, if it is really by Anvari, must have been copied in his youth when he admired the extremely artificial verses of Qatran. Apparently Auhaduddin did not favor the quiet life of a scholar and spent his youth squandering his inherited fortune. When a worthy member of society called him to task for his irresponsible behavior, he answered in an utterly coarse satire that is among his earliest known works. (It is, however, missing from Mudarris Razavi's edition, although it is mentioned in the introduction.)[11] According to legend, Anvari chose to become a panegyrist when he was moved by the sight of a superbly attired man who, it turned out, was a court poet. Anvari then "directed the reins of the horse of intention toward the arena of poetry and snatched the ball of eloquence from the contemporary poets."[12] It is more likely that Anvari's career began after a trip he made from Abivard to Balkh, then on to Sarakhs and Herat; he returned by the same route and on the way was introduced by his maecenas Abu'l-Hasan al-'Imrani to Sanjar, the Seljukid ruler, with whom he remained associated until the king's death in 1157.

The Seljuks, a Turkish tribe, had risen to prominence during the last years of Mahmud of Ghazna (d. 1030), the powerful emperor remembered as the conqueror of northwest India, at whose court in Ghazna the leading poets of the early eleventh century gathered. The Seljuks soon extended their rule over most of Iran, and their leader Tughrul entered Baghdad, the seat of the Abbasid caliph, in 1055. During the short reign of Alp Arslan (1063-72) the Seljukid armies entered Anatolia, which became an important seat of Islamic culture in the following two centuries. After Alp

Arslan's assassination, Malikshah came to power. During this period (1072-92), regarded as the high tide of Seljukid power, the able vizier Nizamulmulk acted as defender of pure Islamic values by founding colleges (*madrasas*) in the important cities of the empire. Scholars like al-Ghazzali (d. 1111), celebrated as the greatest medieval Muslim thinker, were active, and Islamic mysticism flourished, but a relentless fight against the esoteric sect in Islam – the Ismailis – was also going on. Nizamulmulk fell victim to their revenge, and in the same year – 1092 – Malikshah too was killed. By the year 1100 the Seljukid empire was in shambles, but Sanjar, one of Malikshah's sons and ruler of Khorasan since his boyhood, regained power in 1119. His name stands in later Persian poetry parallel to the names of the great pre-Islamic Persian kings Khusrau and Kaiqubad, who served as exemplars of royal glory. Sanjar's first court poet was Amir Mu'izzi, who was accidentally killed by an arrow Sanjar shot during a hunting party; another court poet, Sabir, who served also as an envoy to the neighboring state of Khwarizm, was drowned by the Khwarizmshah Atsiz. Atsiz had rebelled in 1140-41, and one of the few known anecdotes of Anvari's life is connected with Sanjar's expedition against Atsiz's fortress in Hazarasp in 1147: Anvari and Atsiz's court poet, Rashiduddin Vatvat, exchanged political verses tied to arrows, which they shot from one camp to the other. Anvari made a joke about the diminutive Vatvat, whose nickname means "bat." Supposedly the nickname saved Vatvat from Sanjar's revenge; the poet was considered too small to kill.

Another threat to the Seljukid empire came from the Ghorids, who had begun to extend their power over Afghanistan and had sacked Ghazna. 'Ala'uddin Ghori was detained at Sanjar's court for some time, and, while Anvari satirized him, he later wrote some poems on Ghiyathuddin Ghori (whose beautiful mosque in Herat is still partly intact) and on Shihabuddin Ghori, who led successful campaigns into India, reaching as far as Lahore and Multan.

In Sanjar's service Anvari used all his talents; it was during his patron's captivity with the Ghuzz, who had overrun parts of northwestern Iran, that he composed his most famous ode, called by its first translator "The Tears of Khorassan." This long, touching poem, in which the afflicted province implores the ruler of Samarkand for help, was one of the earliest Persian poems known to Western readers. It begins with these lines:

> O morning breeze, when you pass by Samarqand,
> Bring the letter of the people of Khorassan to that Sultan!

and describes the ravages of the Ghuzz, who looted Merv, massacred the inhabitants of Nishapur in 1154, and ruled Khorasan for two years. Only

Herat was spared. In this *qaṣīda*, traditional forms and figures are filled with deep feeling, as when the suffering country cries out:

> Pity, pity those who search now for barley
> While they were formerly too spoiled to eat sugar!
> Pity, pity those who do not find coarse felt
> As much as their bedding was formerly of satin!
> Pity, pity those who are now disgraced
> As much as they were constantly mentioned because of their decency....[13]

Anvari's *qaṣīdas* in praise of Sanjar have become almost proverbial; for an educated Persian to think of Sanjar means to think of this brilliant court poet. But Sanjar is not the only person Anvari eulogized. We know of at least sixty-six people the poet addressed in laudatory poems, although many names cannot be verified from the historical sources. Among those the poet praised were some highborn ladies of the royal household. When Anvari performed the pilgrimage to Mecca after 560 A.H./A.D. 1165 he seems to have stayed for some time in Baghdad and Mosul, for Qutbuddin Maudud Shah Zangi, the atabeg of Mosul, is among those he praised. In a *qaṣīda* written for Zangi, Anvari bids the ruler admire his, the poet's, achievements:

> The lowliest slave of your knowledge is [equal to] a thousand Platos;
> The humblest servant of your line is [equal to] a thousand Alexanders.
> Before your figures the heart of Ptolemy is helpless;
> Before your words of wisdom the heart of [the astronomer] Abu Ma'shar is
>   deficient....[14]

These lines suggest that Anvari felt he was essentially too learned to be a poet. But he was well aware of a scholar's problems and sorrows and therefore also remarked:

> How can anyone realize that this blue-coloured humpback [i.e., the sky]
> Is so passionately fond of annoying men of learning?[15]

Anvari allegedly assured Sanjar that, if he made Anvari his court poet, he "need have no fear of being bored," because of the many areas of expertise the poet could bring to his verse.[16] In this connection Joseph von Hammer-Purgstall commented: "It seems unbelievable that a poetical talent of such strength as Anvari should have devoted his whole life and his whole energy to nothing but such eulogies.... Indeed, it needs such an outspoken talent of panegyrics as Anvari's to compose a praise poem even about some teeth which Nasiruddin Tahir – God knows by which accident! – had lost...."[17] A portion of Hammer-Purgstall's long chapter on Anvari inspired a laudatory remark by Goethe.[18] Anvari himself was

60

not always comfortable with his role as a panegyrist; in one anecdote he describes the plight of the poet whose greed induced him to write for money: he sent a praise poem to a miser, then, after not getting a reward, dispatched a begging poem, and, when this too went unacknowledged, hurled a satire at the stingy one. Finally he placed himself on the man's threshold and, asked why he did so, answered that he was waiting for the man to die so that he could at least sing a dirge and get some money. Poetry, Anvari states, is "like a child whose nurse is greed," and he goes on to an even more vulgar description of this art.[19] Possibly he gave up poetry in the end – at least poetry for worldly purposes. What is perhaps his most touching work, and certainly one of Anvari's best-known short poems, is his final statement, made when a wretched "little lover" asked him whether he was writing *ghazal*, love poetry, and he answered:

> I wrote *ghazal* and praise song and satire only, friend,
> Since lust and greed and anger were all too strong in me:
> That one remained all night long in grief immersed and thought,
> How to describe the tresses, the curls, the lips so sweet;
> The other one was toiling all day in pain, all night:
> Whence, how, from whom and whether some pennies to obtain.
> A tired dog the third one, whose consolation is
> To find somebody's weakness and to abuse him then.
> Since God has these three hungry, these dogs – far may they be! –
> Turned from me in His mercy and made poor me now free,
> How could I sing a *ghazal*, a satire or a praise? ...[20]

Most Western readers agree with Hammer-Purgstall that "the genius of no other Persian poet is more alien to the genius of the West than that of Anvari, who therefore ... is much more difficult to understand and to translate than most other poets."[21] Since Persian panegyrics are written in a highly sophisticated style, bound by monorhyme, which often extends through a hundred verses, and follow strict rules of prosody, special talent is required to make them interesting as well. The poet's task is not to simply give a true account of the virtues and achievements of the person praised, but rather to combine inherited metaphors and hyperbole in new, unexpected ways and to add fresh puns and turns of phrase. As Nizami 'Arudi says in his classic handbook of Persian poetics, *Chahār Maqāla*, the poet must have studied twenty thousand verses of the ancients and ten thousand verses of contemporary authors, must be well versed in medicine, astrology, and the sciences of religion as well as in pastimes such as chess, backgammon, and polo in order to be equipped to improvise a fitting verse upon every possible occasion.[22] The Western reader, lacking a deeper knowledge of Islamic culture as reflected in Persian literature and unfamiliar with the intricate wordplay that is an integral part of Persian poetry, will soon be lost in the highly cerebral verses of an erudite poet like Anvari, who obviously knew not only the Persian tradition, but also classical Arabic poetry. In addition, Anvari had studied philosophy and knew Avicenna well enough to translate certain of his treatises into Persian.[23] But even though uninitiated Western readers have found Anvari's subjects incomprehensible, his works have been appreciated in the East. The Indian scholar-poet Azad Bilgrami considered Anvari's works models of the four-part *qaṣīda*.[24] This complex, stylized poetic form is written according to a clearly prescribed formula. The four parts are the *maṭlaʿ*, the introductory verse, which should immediately catch the listener's attention; the *gurīz*, the transition from the introductory section to the part in praise of the person to whom the poem is dedicated; the *ḥusn-i ṭalab*, an elegant way of asking for a reward; and the final verse, in which, as in the first one, a catching simile or daring image should be used.

The Western reader may feel more for the short narrative poems (*qiṭʿa*), in which the poet shows his very human side. For instance, Anvari was a man who liked a glass of wine:

> I asked for wine, and you gave me stale vinegar,
> Such that, should I drink it, I should rise up at the
>   resurrection like pickled meat....[25]

Once the poet even had to write a poetical apology for vomiting during a party because he was so drunk.[26]

Little is known about Anvari's personal life. In his work he sometimes asks for the company of his friends, but often satirizes his compatriots mercilessly. We know that he suffered at times from worms, and he also complained of gout. This may be the reason for some of his rather unfriendly remarks about the world and its inhabitants. A caustic poem about Anvari's encounters with the citizens of Balkh, although it may not have been written by Anvari himself, indicates that he was not very well liked by his compatriots. Poems about the evils of women are rather frequent, and his latest biographer has deduced from one small, nasty poem that he was probably married.

The most famous story about Anvari, from the last years of his life, concerns his knowledge of astronomy. He had predicted for a certain day, when all the planets would be in conjunction in the sign of Libra, a terrible storm that would be as devastating as the Deluge. Unfortunately, on the day in question the sky was clear and not the slightest breeze blew; in fact, the following months had much less wind than usual, and – understandably – people ridiculed the aged poet for his miscalculation. But some later defenders claimed that the day Anvari named had been the day Jenghiz Khan, who was to destroy the world as a storm of divine wrath, was born. The conjunction of the planets took place in 1185 or 1186, and, although the date of Anvari's death has been a matter of dispute among scholars – almost no two books give the same year – his death may safely be fixed at about 1190. He died, presumably in Balkh, where he is buried.

Most Persian poets claimed to be masters surpassing everyone else. Anvari also asserted that

> The scratching of my pen
> Is the voice of the trumpet of Israfil,

by which he meant that the very sound of his words rouses humanity for the day of Resurrection. But Anvari, like all other Persian poets, used religious imagery rather indiscriminately; little true religious feeling is found in his poetry. Unlike his contemporary Khaqani (d. 1199), the powerful panegyrist of western Iran, he never composed a poem in honor of the Prophet Muhammad. To be sure, there are allusions to God's wondrous powers, and in a late poem on Balkh in which Anvari swears that he had never satirized the learned inhabitants of that city a chain of some twenty anaphoras points to God's miraculousness.[27] But only one full *tauḥīd*, a poem praising God in his unity and unicity, has come down to us, and this poem is interesting more for its unusual rhyme scheme (on the letter *q*) than for its religious content. The poet creates a tour de force of rare words in the Persian-Arabic lexicon while apparently praising

> The One who decrees, not through an instrument but by absolute power....[28]

Anvari lists the first four caliphs in this poem, which is probably sufficient proof that he was a Sunni Muslim – a fact not surprising at the court of a ruler who boasted of being "the Helper of the Abbasid caliph" and was, like his ancestors, a promotor of the Ash'arite form of the Sunni faith. Like other Persian poets, Anvari indulged in the rhetorical play of *taẓādd* (contrast), which is particularly fitting in a work of praise to God, whose kindness and wrath are visible everywhere and show themselves in inexplicable paradoxes:

> He whose wrath gave the stars the power of throwing [meteors] at devils,
> He whose grace gave fire the quality of nourishing salamanders.[29]

God's power is so wonderful that the loveliest stars of heaven can be used to drive away devils (Koran, Sura 72/9), while fire is not only destructive, but makes a pleasant home for the salamander.

The reader can enjoy these sonorous, powerful religious verses, which

63

sometimes sound almost like a mystic's utterances, but he has more difficulty appreciating the panegyrics on worldly rulers and grandees, which are skillfully interwoven with religious allusions. Perhaps the most famous example of this form is a *qit'a* in which Anvari equates the name of Sanjar, with its numerical value of 313, to the 313 prophets before the Prophet Muhammad (see page 117).

Even though a king is not a prophet, his rank is extremely high:

> You are not Yusuf or Jesus or Moses, but among the kings
> You are the ruler with a face like Yusuf, with a hand
>   like Moses, and with breath like Jesus,[30]

which is to say that the young prince being praised is an exemplar of beauty, as Joseph was according to the Koran (Sura 12); that he possesses the White Hand, like Moses (Sura 27/12 a.o.), which came to symbolize miraculous power and generosity; and that his breath is lifegiving, as was Jesus's breath, which could quicken the dead and make clay birds fly (Sura 5/110). The king's "swift-bridled grace" could turn hell into a paradisical lake, and his "heavily stirruped wrath" could transform the well of Zam-zam in Mecca into fire.[31]

Anvari liked to use the Koranic term *ṣarṣar* (the cold wind), and he associated this sign of divine wrath with the powerful armies of his kings. But of course Anvari also praised his masters' beneficence:

> When your hand fills the cloud with the water of generosity,
> The hand of the plane tree breaks from [the weight of the] silver.[32]

The leaves of the plane tree, in Persian always compared to human hands, are unable to contain the rain of coins showered upon them when the honored vizier's generosity transforms raindrops into pieces of silver. In another praise poem the rising sun burns the night, black as aloeswood, in its censer to produce scents for the grandee Anvari is praising.[33]

A poem that shows Anvari's skill, and that was therefore frequently quoted by later critics, is dedicated to Sultan Sanjar and contains in each of its twenty-two verses the mention of the four elements, beginning with the lines:

> The *water* of the eye and the *fire* of the heart carried away the pleasure
>   of my soul
> As a sharp *wind* carries straw from the surface of the *dust* in the wasteland.[34]

Anvari's vocabulary and imagery are full of surprises; he may address a royal princess:

> To sing praise and laud for someone else but you
> Is like performing the ablutions with sand at the seashore.[35]

64

The action described is ritually prohibited, because only when there is no water available may one perform the ablutions before prayer with sand.

The enemies of Anvari's masters are described in equally colorful terms:

> He who wishes you evil has, like the silkworm, spun from the spindle of his
> tongue his own shroud over his head and foot.[36]

The hoof of the prince's horse, however, and the ruby of his headgear fill the world from the earthly dust to the Pleiades.[37]

There are, of course, complaints about life's brevity, about faithlessness and loneliness, intelligently woven into the grand tapestry of the poet's loftiest works:

> Don't desire from them faithfulness, for they
> Are like time: they don't know what faithfulness is.[38]

That idea was restated, but in reverse form, eight centuries later by one of the greatest admirers of Anvari in India, the poet Ghalib (d. 1869), who in an Urdu verse asks his friend to call him back whenever she wants, for:

> I am not time past that I cannot return.

Anvari knew how to express his grief in images that were to become standard expressions in later Persian poetry:

> I jumped up from the place of sleep and sat inside the house,
> A breast full of fire and an eye full of water.[39]

> I shed so many tears that Noah's ark would be drowned;
> I sighed so much that the tents would catch fire.[40]

And in a few words that became proverbial, Anvari satirized the stupidity and pomposity of many of his contemporaries:

> Could everyone who has a rod and an ass
> Be like Moses or like Jesus?[41]

Anvari's poetry was widely read in his time and in the next centuries. We even find allusions to verses and tales from his *Dīvān* in the poetry of the greatest mystical poet who ever wrote in Persian, Maulana Jalaluddin Rumi (1207-73), who grew up in Balkh, where Anvari spent most of his life. Anvari's *qaṣīdas* became models for all later poets, and as late as the nineteenth century the major Persian poets continued to imitate the *zamīn* – the meter and rhyme scheme – of his most famous *qaṣīdas*. The Anvari tradition was particularly strong in India, and as the poet himself had admired Abu'l-Faraj Runi, the poet of Lahore in the late eleventh century, and "liked to look at Abu'l-Faraj's [poetical] garden," his verse, in turn, was loved and admired in the subcontinent. The eighteenth-century polyhistorian-poet Azad Bilgrami mentions that in India he had studied a collection of six *dīvāns* of 676 A.H./A.D. 1277 in which Anvari's and Abu'l-Faraj Runi's poems were copied by the same scribe.[42] This very valuable manuscript may have reached India rather early; the Khudabakhsh Library in Bankipore-Patna possesses several manuscripts dating from the fifteenth century,[43] and in Malwa a commentary on Anvari's *Dīvān* was written shortly after 1500 by one Muhammad ibn Da'ud at the order of Prince Nasiruddin Khilji.[44] A careful study of later Indo-Persian poetry might reveal many allusions and similarities to Anvari. The "incomparable parrot of the branch of knowledge,"[45] as he once modestly called himself, continued to inspire poets up to Ghalib and Muhammad Iqbal (d. 1938).

It seems that the Mughal rulers were particularly fond of Anvari's poetry. In his memoirs Jahangir mentions with pleasure that the poet Naziri (d. 1612), whom he particularly liked, composed an ode in his honor, which was modeled after a well-known *qaṣīda* of the medieval Persian poet. Moreover, when describing a garden party in the summer of 1613, Jahangir exclaimed full of joy that this event was described in Anvari's verse *It's the Day for the Garden,* a poem illustrated in our manuscript (Plate 4). And in his last hour Jahangir's father-in-law, the powerful minister I'timad ad-daula, quoted a fitting verse from Anvari's *Dīvān.*[46]

It is therefore not surprising that a copy of Anvari's work should have been prepared for Akbar. Many of the poet's panegyrics were certainly applicable to rulers other than Sanjar, and the emperor may have enjoyed listening to verses about Samarkand, Merv, and Bukhara, where his own family had lived for centuries.

The copy of the *Dīvān* in the Fogg Art Museum, written in 996 A.H./A.D. 1588 in Lahore by a scribe whose name is unfortunately erased, comprises 354 folios. It measures only 5½ by 2⅞ inches; the text area, surrounded by thin gold and black lines, is 4⅛ by 2 inches. Each page contains fifteen lines of poetry. The first page is missing, as are a number of other pages; there are gaps between folios 92 and 93, 100 and 101, 101 and 102, 107 and 108, 120 and 121, 159 and 160, and 182 and 183 (numbering ours). Between folios 67 and 68 the catchword does not fit, and the sequence of folios 116 to 118 and 154 to 156 is wrong. Folios 108 to 113 have apparently been rewritten, for two miniatures, Plates 2 and 5, do not fit into the textual arrangement in the present order of pages, and repetitions of verses occur both in the present text and on the miniatures; according to the sequence of the rhyme, Plate 5 should precede Plate 2. It is not known whether any of the missing or rewritten pages had a miniature on it, but it is very likely that the small, elegantly calligraphed book had a frontispiece of high quality.

Although the poems are each separated by three-eighths of an inch of space, which is outlined as if for a title, the titles of the poems have not been inserted; we have supplied them from the printed editions.

The inner frame around the text has often pierced the paper so that some text areas are separated from the margins. A number of lower left-hand corners have been repaired. The execution of the manuscript, fine as its calligraphy is, is strangely incoherent: the material for all the textual areas is very fine marbleized paper; the marbleizing – in soft bluish gray, apricot, and darker shades of blue – is sometimes very prominent; at other times it is barely visible, but all the pages have a soft golden patina. The borders are mostly of the same paper, but also of colored, gold-flecked paper, which seems to have been pasted over the brittle original pages. This gold-flecked margin is found on folios 1 through 40, 76 through 80, 169 through 170, 193 through 197, 205 through 212, 230, 233 through 234, 238 through 239, and 337 through 354. The extremely delicate condition of the whole manuscript makes a more thorough investigation impossible.

The copyist of our *Dīvān* has arranged the verses according to the true rhyming letters, not, as usual, according to the last letter of the *radīf,* the prolonged rhyme; thus, a poem rhyming in -*ānast* is classified under *n,* not under *t,* as it is in all modern editions. The *qaṣīdas* end on fol. 212; they are separated from the *qiṭ'as* by a miniature (Plate 7); likewise, the only *mathnavī* of Anvari is separated from the first *ghazal* by a charming ornament with bird motifs (Plate 15). The text of the poems shows slight variations from the latest printed editions; sometimes verses are left out. On the whole it is much closer to Nafisi's edition and contains many of the obscene verses not found in Mudarris Razavi.

The artists of the Fogg manuscript chose to illustrate mainly the second part of the *Dīvān;* only rarely do the *qaṣīdas* offer images that lend themselves to pictures. In almost every case, it is the beginning of a *qaṣīda* or the contents of a *qiṭ'a* that inspired the painters. Among the *qaṣīdas,* the illustrations on fol. 173a (Plate 4), which shows the delights of the garden in spring, and on fol. 110a (Plate 5), in which the excitement of travel is described, are particularly charming. But it was certainly easier for the painters to illustrate the short stories and jokes contained in the second part of the *Dīvān,* even though the artists often reset a rustic scene in a courtly milieu.

67

The Fogg's beautiful "pocket book" of Anvari was completed in the thirty-third year of Akbar's long reign – nine years after the promulgation of the *maḥżar*, the decree by which the emperor was given supreme power in religious matters, and seven years after the introduction of the esoteric Din-i Ilahi, or Divine Faith, the eclectic religious order to which nineteen of Akbar's closest friends belonged. It was the time that 'Urfi of Shiraz and Faizi were competing for the emperor's favors as court poets; 'Urfi claimed to have surpassed Anvari in his work.

It is fitting to quote a verse by Anvari in which he describes Sanjar commanding him to recite his verse. In a sense, Akbar gave the poet the same order when he commissioned a copy of the *Dīvān* for his own library:

> The Lord of the world called Anvari
> Before him, gave him his hand and had him seated,
> Called for wine and asked him for poetry....[47]

NOTES

The two most recent editions of Anvari's poetry are *Dīvān-i-Anvarī*, ed. Sa'id-i Nafisi (Tehran, 1337 sh./A.D. 1958), referred to here as Nafisi; and *Dīvān-i-Anvarī*, ed. Muhammad Taqi Mudarris Razavi, vol. 1, *Qaṣā'id* (Tehran, 1337 sh./A.D. 1958, 2nd ed., 1347 sh./A.D. 1968); vol. 2, *Muqaṭṭa'āt, ghazaliyāt, rubā'iyāt* (Tehran, 1340 sh./A.D. 1961), referred to here as Mudarris Razavi 1 and 2. This edition is expurgated; it does not contain most of the crude or obscene verses included in Nafisi and the Fogg manuscript.

1. Edward Granville Browne, *A Literary History of Persia* (Cambridge, 1902; reissue, 1928), 2:116.

2. Muhammad 'Aufi, *Lubāb al-albāb*, ed. E. G. Browne and Muhammed Qazvini (London, 1902), 2:125; also quoted in Nafisi, introduction, iii.

3. E. G. Browne, *A Literary History of Persia*, 2: 364-94. Browne's statements are based largely on the only full monograph on the Persian poet, by Valentine Zhukovski, *Materials for a Biography and Characteristic Sketch; 'Alī Awḥadu'd-Din Anwarī* (St. Petersburg, 1883);

summarized by Wilhelm Pertsch in *Literaturblatt für Orientalische Philologie* (Leipzig, 1884-85), 2: 16.

4. Hermann Ethé, "Neupersische Literatur," in *Grundriss der iranischen Philologie*, ed. Wilhelm Geiger and Ernst Kuhn (Strasbourg, 1898-1902), 2: 262.

5. Reuben Levy, *Persian Literature. An Introduction* (London, 1923), 42.

6. Jan Rypka, *History of Iranian Literature* (Dordrecht, Netherlands, 1968), 198.

7. Mudarris Razavi, introduction, 123.

8. Alessandro Bausani, "Storia della letteratura neo-persiana," in Antonio Pagliaro and Alessandro Bausani, *Storia della letteratura persiana* (Milan, 1960), 380-98, 576.

9. Arthur John Arberry, *Classical Persian Poetry* (London, 1958), 116.

10. For Qatran, the leading poet of Azerbaijan, d. after A.D. 1072, see Rypka, *History of Iranian Literature*, 194. The problem of this attribution is dealt with in Nafisi, introduction, 28, pls. 1, 2, based on Mehdi Bayani, "Dīvān-i-Qaṭrān be-khaṭṭ-i Anvarī-i Abīvardī," *Yaghmā* 11/3 (1329 sh./A.D. 1950): 445-74.

11. Mudarris Razavi, introduction, 22.

12. Nafisi, introduction, xix, quotes from *Tadhkira-i Ḥusainī* of Mir Hasan Dost Sanbheli.

13. The translation was first published in *The Asiatic Miscellany* (Calcutta, 1785), 286-310; for different versions, see E. G. Browne, *A Literary History of Persia*, 2: 386-89; text in Nafisi, 105-8; Mudarris Razavi, 1: 205-15, no. 82: "From the tongue of the people of Khorasan to the *khaqān* of Samarkand, Ruknuddin Qilich Tamghach Khan, the adopted son of Sultan Sanjar."

14. Nafisi, 111-15; Mudarris Razavi, 1: 213-19, no. 85.

15. E. G. Browne, *A Literary History of Persia*, 2: 377. From a *qaṣīda* devoted to Nasiruddin Tahir. Nafisi, 27-29; Mudarris Razavi, 1: 41-45, no. 18.

16. E. G. Browne, *A Literary History of Persia*, 2: 375.

17. Joseph von Hammer-Purgstall, *Geschichte der schönen Redekünste Persiens* (Vienna, 1818), 97-98; the text in Nafisi, 337; Mudarris Razavi, 2: 559, no. 90.

18. In Goethe's *West-Oestlicher Divan* (Stuttgart, 1819), the "Buch der Sprüche" contains a short poem inspired by Hammer-Purgstall's positive assessment:

> Enweri sagt's, ein herrlichster der Männer,
> Des tiefsten Herzens, höchsten Hauptes
>   Kenner:
> "Dir frommt an jedem Ort, zu jeder Zeit
> Geradheit, Urteil und Verträglichkeit."

(Quoth Anvari, one of the most glorious men,
acquainted with the deepest [secrets of] the heart as well
as with the highest head [i.e., the nobility]:
In every place and at every time
Directness, sound judgment, and suavity are fitting.)

At about the same time, in the early 1820s, the German orientalist and poet Friedrich Rückert composed an oriental encomium inspired by Anvari: "Orientalisches Loblied, nach dem Persischen des Enweri."

19. Nafisi, 457; Mudarris Razavi, 2: 724, no. 428; for a description of poetry as the "menstruation of men," which is no longer fitting after the age of fifty, see Nafisi, 448; Mudarris Razavi, 2: 713, no. 407.

20. Nafisi, 423; Mudarris Razavi, 2: 694, no. 367; quoted in full in Jami, *Baháristan* (Lucknow, 1875), rauda 7; 98.

21. J. von Hammer-Purgstall, *Geschichte*, 99.

22. Nizami 'Arudi, *Revised Translation of the Chahár Maqála ("Four Discourses") of Nizámí-i-Arūḍī*, trans. E. G. Browne (London, 1921), 32; for Persian text and commentary, see Nizami 'Arudi, *Chahár Maqála*, ed. Muhammed Qazvini (London, 1910).

23. See Mudarris Razavi, introduction, 98; but Avicenna is also criticized implicitly in our fol. 243a.

24. Azad Bilgrami, *Khizāna-i 'āmira* (Lucknow, 1871), 8-10. Anvari is the first poet mentioned in this eighteenth-century biographical dictionary of India.

25. E. G. Browne, *A Literary History of Persia*, 2: 379.

26. Nafisi, 463; Mudarris Razavi, 2: 740, no. 458.

27. The poem, a *saugandnāma* (Nafisi, 304; Mudarris Razavi, 1: 469-75, no. 190), contains this beautiful line about God:

> He, whose name is the first line on the tablet of the tongues:
> This one calls him [in Arabic] *ilāh*, that one [in Persian] *īzad*, and that other one [in Turkish] *tanrī*....

28. Nafisi, 174-76; Mudarris Razavi, 1: 272-74, no. 107, a prayer poem.

29. In the *saugandnāma* cited in n. 27.

30. Nafisi, 327; Mudarris Razavi, 1: 505, no. 205, without the name of the addressee.

31. Nafisi, 199; Mudarris Razavi, 1: 336-38, no. 131. "In praise of 'Imaduddin Piruz Shah and Khwaja Jalal al-vuzara [Jalaluddin 'Umar ibn Mukhlis]."

32. Nafisi, 228; Mudarris Razavi, 1: 349-51, no. 137. In praise of the *ṣadr* (chief) Tajuddin Ibrahim.

33. Nafisi, 21-22; Mudarris Razavi, 1: 19-21, no. 9. In praise of Abu'l-Ma'ali Majduddin ibn Ahmad, with the *radīf* (recurrent rhyme word) *āftāb* ("sun").

34. Nafisi, 125-26; Mudarris Razavi, 1: 190-91, no. 78.

35. Nafisi, 201-2; Mudarris Razavi, 1: 341-42, no. 133. About Princess Radiyatuddin Maryam.

36. Nafisi, 285-86; Mudarris Razavi, 1: 441-43, no. 179. In praise of Jalaluddin Ahmad-i Mukhlis.

37. Nafisi, 281-82; Mudarris Razavi, 1: 433-34, no. 174, without a name.

38. Nafisi, 521 (*ghazal*); not included in Mudarris Razavi.

39. Nafisi, 19-21; Mudarris Razavi, 1: 29-31, no. 13. In praise of Nasiruddin Tahir.

40. Nafisi, 144-46; Mudarris Razavi, 1: 165-68, no. 71. In praise of Sahib Sa'id Jalal al-vuzara 'Umar ibn Mukhlis.

41. Nafisi, 84-86; Mudarris Razavi, 1: 123-27, no. 56. In praise of Sahib Sadr Tahir ibn Muzaffar.

42. Azad Bilgrami, *Khizāna-i 'āmira*, 8; the other poets are Zahir Faryabi, Shamsuddin Tabasi, Nasir-i Khusrau, and 'Abdul 'aziz Lisani, whose poems are in Arabic.

43. *Catalogue of the Arabic and Persian Manuscripts in the Oriental Public Library at Bankipore* (Calcutta, 1908-46), 1: nos. 25-27.

44. Bibliothèque Nationale, Département des manuscrits, *Catalogue des manuscrits persans de la Bibliothèque Nationale.* Vol. 2 of *Catalogue des manuscrits persans par E. Blochet* (Paris, 1905-34), 556.

45. In a *qaṣīda* for the *khaqān* Piruz Shah. Nafisi, 26-27; Mudarris Razavi, 1: 38-40, no. 17.

46. Jahangir, *The Tūzuk-i Jahāngīrī; or Memoirs of Jahāngīr*, trans. Alexander Rogers, ed. Henry Beveridge (London, 1909-14), 2: 222.

47. Nafisi, 373.

PAGES

FROM THE DIVAN

PLATE ONE

The Beloved Arrives at Midnight

Attributed to Shiva Das

The miniatures in this Dīvān transport us into the Mughal world – in this instance, into a small bedchamber of the sort seen to this day in Akbar's greatest architectural complex, Fathpur-Sikri. As conjured up by Shiva Das, the room's stone walls are coated with lime, polished to resemble white marble, and decorated with arabesque flowering vines. Niches containing glass bottles, a glowing lamp, and a charpoi, or bed, are the few amenities of the characteristically stark Mughal room in which the artist has set his nocturnal tryst. Costumes, too, are of the Akbar period. One wonders, however, if turbans were worn in bed.

Two miniatures by Shiva Das for the British Library's Dārābnāma (fols. 18a, 126a) suggest that painting pleasing young faces was the artist's forte.

Fols. 53 and 54a contain the second half of a poem in praise of the grand vizier Nasiruddin Abu'l-Fath Tahir ibn Muzaffar,[1] which begins with the lines:

> Drunk from my nightly wine, I had fallen down unconscious
> Last night in my room, when my beloved knocked at my door.

Nasiruddin, the grandson of the famous Seljukid statesman Nizamulmulk, was Sultan Sanjar's last vizier. Appointed to office in 528 A.H./A.D. 1134, he was killed by the Ghuzz in 548 A.H./A.D. 1153. Anvari wrote more than thirty poems in his honor.

The miniature illustrates the beginning of the following *qaṣīda*, composed in honor of Khwaja Ziya'uddin Maudud Ahmad-i 'Isami, a high-ranking official in Herat, to whom Anvari dedicated several poems.[2]

Close to me came	the Sun of the Lovely at night,
Tall as a cypress,	a face like the radiant moon.
Thousands of souls	aflame through his ruby lips,
Thousands of hearts	caught in the snare of his tress.

1. Nafisi, 118-21; Mudarris Razavi, 1: 205-20, no. 83.
2. Nafisi, 162-64; Mudarris Razavi, 1: 250-53, no. 97.

بر مرکز مراد تو ایّام را مدار   تا چرخ را مدار بود گردد این مدار

جوینده رضای تو سلطان دلبخش   دارنده بقای تو سلطان دادگر

بر من آمد خورشید نیکون اشبکه   بعد چو سرو بلند و رخ چو بدر منیر

PLATE TWO

Anvari Entertains in a Summer House

Attributed to Basawan

Although the old poet might not have enjoyed climbing into a tree platform, Basawan, to whom we attribute this miniature on the grounds of style, avoided illustrating Anvari's description of the actual ascent by painting the loveliest summer retreat he could imagine. Doubtless it reminded Akbar of a similar setting, as painted by 'Abdussamad, in which he as a child conversed with his father, Emperor Humayun. Basawan, a pupil of 'Abdussamad, became – along with Daswanth – one of Akbar's most admired Hindu artists. Gifted with a playwright's insight into personalities, he is also noted for his handling of three-dimensional space, extraordinary treatment of gold, and painterly delight in brushwork. The sensible spit upon which a young attendant turns a piece of meat while fanning the fire is observed with Basawan's usual compelling realism. [1]

Here the poet presents a *qaṣīda* in praise of Khwaja Auhaduddin Ishaq, a little-known personage from Merv. [2]

At first the miniature and its text seem to belong to fol. 114. However, if that were the case, the picture would occupy a verso side, because fol. 115a contains the continuation of a poem that appears in the miniature itself. In the manuscript these two lines are also found at the bottom of the previous page (fol. 114b), following the last ten verses of a *qaṣīda* in praise of Nasiruddin Tahir, the same poem that precedes the miniature on fol. 54a. On the back of the present miniature, which must be a recto side, we find fourteen verses of a sixteen-verse *qaṣīda* in praise of Princess Safvatuddin Maryam Khatun. [3] These fit better into the context because of their rhyme scheme. Thus, Plate 2 is part of the same group of rewritten poems as Plate 5. The group was apparently inserted into a sequence using the rhyme letter *r* without regard for repetitions. The rewritten pages seem to be from the same period as the original; the paper and lettering are almost identical.

The poem accompanying the miniature, written in a light, pleasant style, begins with a charming description of the poet's nightly carousing:

I came, quite drunk, into my house last night
And had with me a loyal, pleasant friend;
And I discovered on the windowsill
A half full bottle of my nightly wine:
Pure as the promises of loving friends
And bitter like the lives of those who love....

The poet then describes how he and his friend entered a summer house and sat close to a window through which a small slice of the horizon was visible. Some

1. Arthur Upham Pope, ed., *A Survey of Persian Art from Prehistoric Times to the Present* (Oxford, 1938-39), 5: pl. 912.
2. Nafisi, 176-78; Mudarris Razavi, 1: 269-71, no. 106.
3. Nafisi, 174; Mudarris Razavi, 1: 268-69, no. 105.

books of logic lay to the right and a few pages of geometry to the left. The whole place was illuminated by the friend's shining face and by the wine. The "sugar of union" was like sweetmeats for them, while the "blood of separation" filled their wine cups. The pair had no need for "swift-fingered singers" or "silver-legged cupbearers"; the poet recited his own verses and accompanied himself. Suddenly the moon rose to fill the room with light and became a partner in the conversation, which turned on fate. In the very middle of the poem the name of Auhaduddin Ishaq is mentioned. The encomium to Ishaq begins after twenty-two verses filled with elegant puns.

PLATE THREE

A Magnanimous Vizier

Attributable to Manohar

So *accurately do these miniatures describe Mughal court life that one wonders if the vizier and his attendants are not actual portraits of officials at the imperial capital. Manohar, to whom we assign this picture as a youthful work, was the son of Basawan, who painted the preceding miniature. He was of the same age as Akbar's eldest son, the art-loving Prince Salim, who probably encouraged Manohar's particularly fine characterizations and detailed still-life studies of account books, glassware, and coffers. The interior shown here, with its markedly European perspective, was probably traced from a European print. Such exotic works were collected by Salim, who later came to the throne as Emperor Jahangir. Many sheets from the prince's collection were mounted in superb borders and bound into sumptuous albums along with Mughal and Iranian miniatures and calligraphies. An album in Leningrad contains Manohar's copy of a print by Georg Pencz, the sixteenth-century German "Little Master."[1] The Mughal painter's work is so accurate that at first sight it appears to be the original engraving.*

Fol. 128a contains a *qaṣīda* in praise of the vizier Khwaja Sadruddin Muhammad, called Nizamulmulk II.[2] He was the son of Nasiruddin Tahir, to whom the preceding *qaṣīda* is devoted.[3]

The poem lacks the usual long descriptive introduction and sets in immediately with highflown praise for the well-blessed Nizamulmulk. The pure heart of his namesake, the prophet Muhammad, assures his continued good fortune. The vizier is called so powerful and glorious that he

> measures the sky's circumference with reason's foot,
> And with the light of good judgment discerns the shadow play of life's tricks;
> [He is a leader] beside whose power the realm of a star seems lowly,
> And before whose penetrating wisdom the tongue of proof is dumb;
> In whose wrath are implied distress, misfortune, and death
> And in whose kindnesses are hidden long life, fortune, and prosperity.
> Possibly God has rendered to the tribunal of his kindness and wrath
> The book of souls and the fate of termination [the judgment of who will be
>   saved and who will be doomed to damnation].
> Thanks to his glory and power, the lion of the tapestry of his hall claws the Leo
>   of the sky;
> Thanks to his magnificence, the quail digs out the hawk's eye;
> Thanks to his strength, the fox tears out the lion's claws....

1. A. A. Ivanov, T. V. Grek, and O. F. Akimushkin, *Al'bom indiyskikh i persiskikh miniatyur XVI-XVIII vv.* (The Album of Indian and Persian Miniatures of the 16th-18th Centuries) (Moscow, 1962), pl. 20.
2. Nafisi, 189-92; Mudarris Razavi, 1: 280-82, no. 111.
3. Nafisi, 184-86; Mudarris Razavi, 1: 294-97, no. 117.

بنور رای تصویر کند خیال حال   بکام عقل مساحت کند محیط فلک

The poet continues in this vein for another twenty-six verses that contain a breathtaking torrent of puns and other plays on words, as well as antitheses and hyperboles. Anvari ends with a wish:

> May your enemy's star never reach its ascendancy and zenith!
> May the constellation of your own fortune never see decline and nadir!

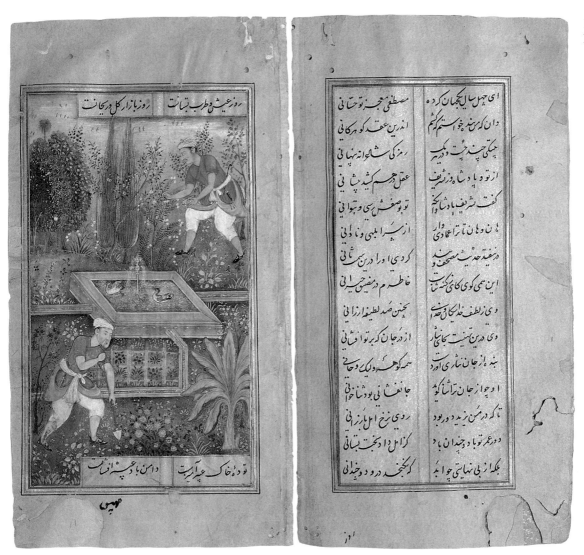

PLATE FOUR

It's the Day for the Garden!

Attributed to Mahesh

Throughout the Mughal dynasty's three-century history in India, its emperors were avid lovers of gardens. Like their paintings, their gardens reflected the rulers' moods and tastes. Mahesh's version, with its waterways, ducks, and spontaneous asymmetry, typifies the easy humanity of Akbar's court, especially as compared to the hushed formality of the famed gardens at the Taj Mahal, designed for his grandson, Shah Jahan (r. 1628-58). Akbar's trees and flowers grow with natural abandon, whereas Shah Jahan's appear to have been set with a jeweler's precision.

Mahesh was one of the seventeen artists of Akbar's ateliers singled out for special mention by Akbar's friend and biographer, Abu'l-Fazl.[1] Here we see the painter at his most lyrically appealing, a dashing brush handler whose flowers sparkle like fireworks.

Fol. 172b contains the second half of a *qaṣīda* in praise of Majduddin Abu'l-Hasan al-'Imrani "when the Sultan bestowed a robe of honor upon him."[2]

'Imrani, who lived most of the time in Sarakhs, was a special benefactor of Anvari. It was probably he who introduced the poet to Sultan Sanjar, because he was for many years one of the most influential members of Sanjar's entourage. Anvari devoted both long praise poems and shorter laudatory fragments to him. In later years, 'Imrani was imprisoned and was finally killed in 545 A.H./A.D. 1150-51; Anvari composed a dirge for him.

The next poem, whose beginning is on the miniature itself, is also dedicated to 'Imrani:[3]

It's the day for the garden, for cheer and for joy;
It's the day for the market of basil and rose.
The dust is all mixed with amber and musk;
The skirt of the zephyr spreads fragrance and scents.

1. Abu'l-Fazl, *A'īn-i Akbarī*, trans. H. Blochmann (Calcutta, 1873), 1: 108.
2. Nafisi, 312-14; Mudarris Razavi, 1: 485-87, no. 196.
3. Nafisi, 57-59; Mudarris Razavi, 1: 79-82, no. 34.

روز عیش و طرب بستانست
روز بازار گل و ریحانست
توده خاک عبیرآمیز است
دامن باد عبیرافشانست

PLATE FIVE

The Poet's Journey
Probably by 'Abdussamad

Sunlight *breaks through the clouds in this appealing landscape with its reful-*
gently "golden" boulder and animal-like rock grotesques. We are invited to walk
through its valleys and fields, toward the distant town, prickly with temple spires
and pleasure domes. It is the most convincing aerial perspective in the Dīvān *as*
well as the earliest precisely datable achievement of this sort in all Mughal art.
This image is particularly complex and finely painted; its rhythms, coloring, and
figures are probably by 'Abdussamad. Underneath their Mughal naturalism,
many passages hint at the painter's Iranian past.

With appealing sensitivity, the artist trailed the marbleized shapes of the
border into vistas and clouds, enhancing the gently poetic mood and lending
additional mystery to "the globe of dust and . . . sky."

The exact position of this miniature cannot be established. It was probably near
fol. 110 in the original sequence. It must be a verso, yet the *qaṣīda* connected with it
appears on a recto side and continues without interruption to its end. The verso side
of the miniature also contains this same poem, underscoring the name of the
official to whom it is dedicated by devoting an extra line to his name. It does not
relate at all to the present arrangement of pages and seems to belong to the same
group of rewritten and misplaced pages as Plate 2. According to the rhyme scheme,
this poem should precede that folio.

The *qaṣīda* is dedicated to Sahib Sa'id Muhammad, the *mīr-āb* ("superinten-
dent of the river") of Merv.[1] The first part of the poem deals with the poet's journey,
speaks of the importance of traveling, and concludes with these lines:

> Man has no honor in his native land;
> A gem is worthless in its native mine.
> Look at the globe of dust and at the sky:
> The earth, you see, is low through restfulness.
> Through constant journey is the sky so high!
> If trees could move and wander far away,
> They would not suffer from the ax or saw!

This last line was borrowed, with a slight change, by Maulana Jalaluddin Rumi
(d. 1273), who used it as the beginning of his famous mystical poem about the
importance of the spiritual journey.[2]

---

1. Nafisi, 121-23, says the work is dedicated to Khwaja Sadruddin Mahmud; Mudarris Razavi, 1: 219-21,
no. 84.
2. Maulana Jalaluddin Rumi, *Dīvān-i kabīr*, ed. Badi 'uzzaman Furuzanfar (Tehran, 1336 sh./A.D. 1957), 3,
no. 1142.

PLATE SIX

You Make Sweet Life Increase

Even "ripe" pictures of the Akbar period often contain clues of their artist's pre-Mughal style through lingering formulas for figures, trees, architecture, and ornament. Here, the otherworldly Khwaja Mansur's angularly jutting limbs and poses hark back to the anonymous painter's origins in the so-called Chaurapanchasika style, with its bold simplifications and expressive but formulized characterizations.[1] On the other hand, the artist shows himself to be an up-to-date Akbari painter of distinction, capable of making fine portraits and projecting airy three-dimensionality. We admire his throng of beggars, clamoring for Mansur's favors with well-mannered eagerness.

Fols. 208b and 209a contain a *qaṣīda* "in praise of Khwaja Mansur" and a description of the Mansuriyya palace and garden as well as a praise poem for Nasiruddin Tahir, the grand vizier:[2]

> How incredible [you are], you garden and you palace of Mansur!
> Perhaps you are a heaven sent by God into the world?
> Even if you are not paradise – you are surely *not* of this world,
> For this world makes life diminish,
>   and you make sweet life increase....

The poet then describes the bluish green pond, which looks like a sky in the depths of the earth, and the jewel-like watercourse. Only paradisical metaphors are used: the lips of the garden's roses smile; its nightingale fears no separation; the shade of the foliage of its trees is like the shade of the Huma-bird – which grants a kingdom to anyone it touches; the shadow of its lofty palace cannot be measured by the "yardstick of day and night." The garden is then asked to kiss the vizier's hand with the lips of rosebuds; to kindle the censer of red, flamelike buds; to bruise ambergris in the mortar of the tulips; and to make doves and nightingales sing like a joyous chorus at the vizier's feast.

1. Leela Shiveshwarkar, *The Pictures of the Chaurapañchāśikā, a Sanskrit Love Lyric* (New Delhi, 1967).
2. Nafisi, 294-95, "in praise of Khwaja Mansur"; Mudarris Razavi, 1: 443-45, no. 180.

PLATE SEVEN

Anvari's Requests Are Brought

97

Six amiable, courtly figures arrive, bearing goods. Their eyes are upturned – a device that implies the poet's presence in an imaginary miniature on the facing page. We share Anvari's sense of anticipation, for the tightly packed bundles and cloth-covered tray are promisingly weighty. Surely such an elegantly dressed delegation could bring only delights!

Here, in jewel-like scale, we see the bulging amplitude of form so characteristic of Mughal painting, a fullness that brings to mind succulently ripe fruit and is also an essential characteristic of all Indian art.

Fol. 213b contains the end of a *qaṣīda* in honor of the *sayyid as-sādāt* (leader of the descendants of the prophet) Khwaja Majduddin Ja'far-i 'Alavi, who belonged to a leading Nishapuri family and who was praised by many poets.[1]

This small picture separates the last *qaṣīda* in the *Dīvān* from the first *qiṭ'a*. *Qiṭ'as* are short, topical poems in which praise, coarse satire, more or less serious advice, jokes, or the poet's requests for wine, ice, white paper, a cotton shirt, or other amenities are expressed. *Qiṭ'as* are also used for chronograms. In our manuscript a few short *qaṣīdas* written for special purposes are included in the *qiṭ'a* section.

The first *qiṭ'a* is called "A Word of Wisdom and Advice."[2] This poem is a typical display of Anvari's learned style and contains clever allusions to the Koran as well as references to history and legend.

The poet warns a friend not to "knock at the door of unattainable desires" and then quotes Sana'i, the famous religious poet of Ghazna (d. about 1131), who asked God to bless him so that his splendor (*sanā*) might become so great that it would make Avicenna jealous. (In medieval Persian poetry that philosopher symbolized intellectualism as opposed to mystical spirituality and true religious feeling.) The poet's friend is further admonished that the "Gog of desire" is powerless against the iron dam of God's will. This is an allusion to a story in the Koran (Sura 18/94-96) that tells of Alexander building a copper wall at the end of the world; the wall cannot be pierced by Gog or Magog. The poet ends by reminding his friend that one end of the rope of success is in man's hand thanks to God's order to "strive" (*jāhidū*). However, as the Koran states, striving will be useless unless it is combined with devotion ("in us"; *fīnā*): "As for those who strive in us, we surely guide them to our paths" (Sura 29/69).

The facing page contains a short *qaṣīda* telling of the sage who followed Nasiruddin Tahir to Mansuriyya, but was barred from entering the garden where the vizier's party was being held. He then recited a poem requesting admission.[3]

1. Nafisi, 288-89; Mudarris Razavi, 1: 507-8, no. 207.
2. Nafisi, 322-23; Mudarris Razavi, 2: 512, no. 4.
3. Nafisi, 1; Mudarris Razavi, 2: 513, no. 5.

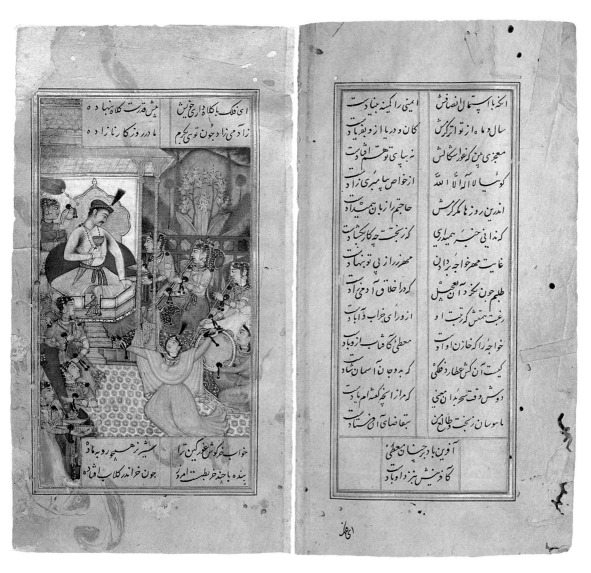

PLATE EIGHT

Heavenly Joys Come to Earth
Attributed to Khem Karan

Lively, attentive Rajput girls engage our ears and eyes with tambourine, flute, vina, and thudding heels. We share the royal patron's delight as he gazes piercingly into a serving girl's eyes. We also muse at the hypnotic symmetry of the contrastingly silent landscape suggestive of a large face — that of another unexpected guest at a jolly party.

The atmosphere of this miniature evokes Akbar's physicality and good humor. It is not surprising, therefore, that Khem Karan was one of the artists singled out from hundreds in the imperial workshop by Abu'l-Fazl, who doubtless reflected the emperor's enthusiasm in his choice. The bounding composition is enhanced by a carefully chosen sheet of marbleized paper containing forms as highly charged as the miniature's transcendent levity. A Hindu, Khem Karan personified Abu'l-Fazl's comment that "their pictures surpass our conception of things." [1] *Although this miniature is the least stylistically progressive in the Dīvān, it is the most visionary.*

Fol. 242b contains the end of a long *qiṭʻa* in which Anvari thanks Majduddin Abu'l-Hasan al-ʻImrani for a gift. [2]

Fol. 243a contains a *qiṭʻa* called "He Wants Wine":

Oh you, before whose might the sky
    took off its mighty crown —
Mother Fate has never borne
    a man more generous than you....

The poet, after a complicated pun on the names of animals, complains that today he is like a donkey mired in mud with a gaggle of geese. Then, continuing his punning, he turns to a flattering description of the pleasant company he finds himself in, which includes houris of paradise, "before whose coral lips intellect stands up, attracted like straw to rosy amber." The poet concludes by thanking the patron who has arranged for so many lovely things — although he has failed to supply wine — and ends with an obscene remark. [3]

1. Abu'l-Fazl, *A'īn-i Akbarī,* 1: 107.
2. Nafisi, 340-41; Mudarris Razavi, 2: 529-30, no. 45.
3. Nafisi, 449-50; not included in Mudarris Razavi.

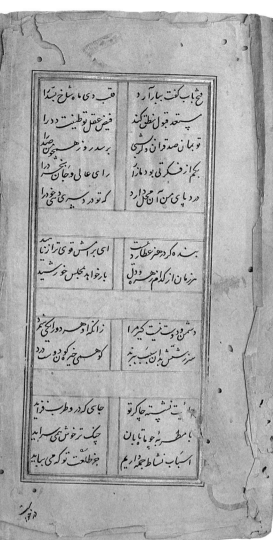

PLATE NINE

Firing up the Poet's Kettle

Attributed to Nanha, whose name can be deciphered in the border

More than any other Akbari artist, Nanha makes one feel the muscular strain of hard work. Carrying, stirring, kneading, and breaking are all depicted here with such emphatic gestures that we join in the preparation of the poet's not very lavish meal. Nanha's style is unmistakable. In his miniatures, including at least ten in the Dārābnāma,[1] boldly simple outlines, massively rounded modeling, and ruggedly vital rhythms generate bustling monumentality. Whereas most of Akbar's painters failed to ground their figures, Nanha's stand with authority, due to their weighty lower legs and ankles, thick as tree trunks. Despite their almost elephantine proportions and thick skin, his figures have delicately mobile hands, feet, and faces. Fingers grip, toes flex, and eyes focus. Nanha was also a deft portraitist.

Fol. 246b contains the continuation of a *qiṭ'a*. Anvari has had some pain in his foot, and Nasiruddin Tahir, the grand vizier, has come to visit him. The *qiṭ'a* is his apology for his ill health.[2] There follows a *qiṭ'a* in excuse for some mistake,[3] an obscene *qiṭ'a*,[4] and a *qiṭ'a* that continues on fol. 247a, called "He Requests the Presence of a Friend":[5]

> Your servant sits here in a place,
> A place where joys increase:
> A singing girl (a radiant moon!)
> Plays on her harp sweet tunes.
> All that we need for happiness
> Is here – except your face.
> Therefore we two implore you, friend:
> Please join us; please come soon!

The miniature apparently belongs to the next *qiṭ'a*, "Request for Kindling." The poet needs firewood so that he may again hear the noise of his little kettle, which has stopped boiling for want of wood.

1. The figure stirring the pot here is almost identical to one by Nanha in the British Library manuscript (MS Or. 4615, fol. 24a).
2. Nafisi, 330; Mudarris Razavi, 2: 516, no. 12.
3. Nafisi, 397; Mudarris Razavi, 2: 645, no. 25.
4. Nafisi, 373; not included in Mudarris Razavi.
5. Nafisi, 411; Mudarris Razavi, 2: 635, no. 245.
6. Nafisi, 453; Mudarris Razavi, 2: 718, no. 418.

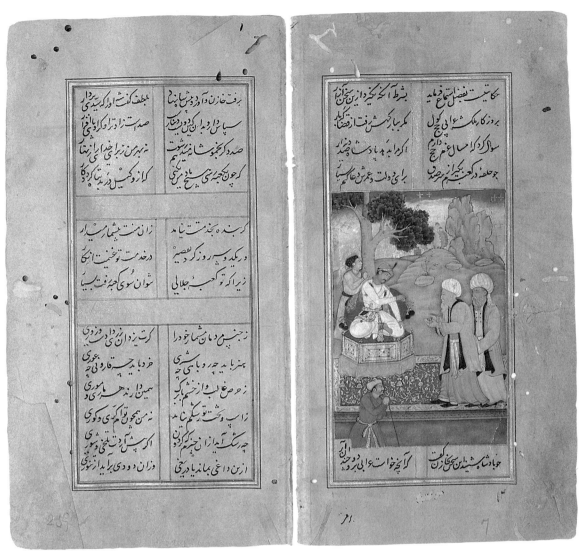

PLATE TEN

Malikshah's Double Gift

Distant rocks almost look heavenward in amused disgust over the "middle-man," at once so generously and roughly treated by Malikshah. The stodgy gentleman, with his covetous hands – their fingers like talons ready for a kill – gives us a clear idea of the sort of person Akbar did not like. Is he the actual likeness of a leader of the orthodoxy so opposed to the emperor, and, in return, so ridiculed, threatened, yet – usually – tolerated by him? Malikshah, enthroned, strongly resembles Akbar, and the figure is probably intended as a portrait. Artists often honored their patrons by depicting them in noble or heroic roles.

The dark stains under Malikshah's arms represent perfumed oil, or 'iṭr, probably made from musk and other delicious scents.

Fol. 258b contains a *qiṭ'a* called "Anecdote About Malikshah, Sultan Sanjar's Father, and a Bedouin":[1]

> Here is a story. Listen to it please,
> Provided that you do not take offence!
> When Malikshah was king, a bedouin
> Thought of a pilgrimage; he came to him
> And said, "I want to go on pilgrimage –
> And if the king would give a hundred bucks
> I'd pray intensely for his health and reign
> When I sincerely grasp the Ka'ba's door!"
> The king heard it and said: "Oh, treasurer,
> Give this man twice as much as he's asked for!"
> Off went the treasurer and brought the gold.
> The king said kindly: "Take it! Hurry up!
> Look well – there are two hundred gold dinars –
> One hundred are for food and lodging, friend;
> One hundred are a secret bribe from me
> (Not for my sake, nay, rather for God's sake!)
> That, reaching there, you will *not* mention me –
> For such a middleman would spoil my cause!"

On fol. 259a is Anvari's short excuse for not visiting someone and the beginning of a poem in which the poet maligns a "worldly person."[2]

1. Nafisi, 408; Mudarris Razavi, 2: 648-49, no. 265.
2. Nafisi, 649; Mudarris Razavi, 2: 649, no. 266. Nafisi, 466-67; Mudarris Razavi, 2: 742, no. 460.

PLATE ELEVEN

Ladies Witnessing Suggestive Donkeys

How coarsely funny dared an artist be at Akbar's court? This miniature might represent the outer limit, for we have seen no more explicit pictures of this period. Decorously jeweled and betasseled ladies have strayed from the harem – and face the consequences. Stretching into the distance, a landscape includes a cubistic town, indianized from a European source by the addition of rooftop pavilions – delightful, airy places to relax and converse. The hound in the foreground is more amused by the women than by the unseemly asses.

Fol. 261b contains the end of a satire against the *qāḍī* of Merv,[1] a *qiṭ'a*, "Asking for the Presence of a Friend,"[2] and a *qiṭ'a* in which Anvari asks his host's forgiveness for his misbehavior in a state of utter drunkenness.[3] There follows – continued onto the miniature of fol. 262a and its verso – a *qiṭ'a* called "Joke":[4]

> One day some women from the upper class
> Went to the meadows for a little walk.
> While they were lingering there a while they saw
> A group of donkeys grazing in the fields.
> A male showed longing for a jenny-ass,
> Just like a lover for a pretty girl....

The women, marveling at the male donkey's intense treatment of the female, express in most vulgar terms their disappointment with their husbands' performances.

1. Nafisi, 407; not included in Mudarris Razavi.
2. Nafisi, 446; Mudarris Razavi, 2: 725, no. 431.
3. Nafisi, 466; Mudarris Razavi, 2: 738, no. 454.
4. Nafisi, 441; not included in Mudarris Razavi.

PLATE TWELVE

An Interlude of Birds

Although this gratifying little picture precedes verses referring to assorted birds, it is less an illustration than a reminder of one of the constant pleasures of Indian life. Indoors and out, birds flutter colorfully, freely, and often noisily. Here, three seem "caged" by the rectangular frame and look longingly toward their golden friends who enjoy freedom in the delightfully ornamented borders.

Fol. 307b contains the end of the *qiṭʿa* that is probably the most famous of Anvari's panegyrics for Sultan Sanjar. The poet states that the numerical value of the name Sanjar, 313 (s=60, n=50, j=3, r=200), represents the 313 God-sent prophets. However, if someone else named Sanjar should claim the same honor, he is advised to recite the Koranic statement *wa ūlī'l-amr minkum* (Sura 4/59): "Obey God, and obey the Messenger and *those of you* who have authority." Because the word *minkum* ("of you") has the same numerical value as *Sulṭān*, 150 (m=40, n=50, k=20, m=40, and s=60, l=30, ṭ=9, a=1, n=50), Sultan Sanjar is singled out. The poem ends with a blessing for the king.[1]

Another *qiṭʿa* follows. The person being praised is one Husamuddin Hasan, from whom Anvari requests a cloak and a pair of shoes, for, as he states after much flattery, it is not fitting that he, the "parrot of poetry," walk barefoot in the clay like a chick. He asks for special footwear and a particular type of coat so that he may look like a partridge – noted in Persian poetry for its elegant gait – or a radiant peacock, and may then put the collar of gratitude around his neck like a ring dove and sing the praise of the donor like a nightingale.[2] There follows a short topical *qaṣīda*.[3]

1. Nafisi, 438; Mudarris Razavi, 2: 599, no. 378.
2. Nafisi, 445; Mudarris Razavi, 2: 706, no. 394.
3. Nafisi, 10; Mudarris Razavi, 1: 8, no. 4.

PLATE THIRTEEN

The Fox's Fear

Attributed to Miskin

119

The artist has contrived a vibrant, scintillating landscape, a perfect setting for leaping foxes, galloping huntsman, birds, and an eager hound. Soaring cliffs, rocks, trees, and flowering bushes seem tremulously vital, recalling Abu'l-Fazl's claim that Akbar's painters made "even inanimate objects look as if they had life." Painted in broad strokes, though on a minuscule scale, the charged brushwork recalls the swinging arcs of the painter's nimble fingers.

Miskin specialized in painting sleek animals in seethingly organic mountainscapes. Although many of his paintings are known, none surpasses the lyricism of this spritely composition, which retains many of the lively qualities of earlier Akbari art. The artist appears to have admired it, too, for the borders, usually assigned to a specialist in ornament, can also be attributed to him. The sinuous, long-tailed simurgh at the upper left and the deer, hare, birds, and craggy rocks amplify the painted world of the miniature. Such passages echo those in Shah Tahmasp's manuscripts and must have been inspired by the example of 'Abdussamad and Mir Sayyid-'Ali. Like all other Safavid elements, these have been fully adapted to the Mughal idiom.

Fol. 313b contains the end of a *qiṭ'a* in which the poet asks for a pair of sandals and a *qiṭ'a* about contentment and freedom.[1]

Fol. 314a contains a *qiṭ'a* called "Complaint About His Contemporaries":[2]

A fox was running, grieving for his life.
Another fox saw him in such a state
And asked: "Please tell me, brother, what is wrong?"
He said: "The king is hunting donkeys here!"
"But you are not a donkey – so why fear?"
He answered: "That is right; but, oh!, these men;
They do not know and they cannot discern.
They think that fox and donkey are the same!"

A similar story is found in Jalaluddin Rumi's *Mathnavī* (Book 5, ll. 2447ff.). The poet tells of a man who fled because the king was hunting wild asses, until someone told him that he was not an ass (a symbol of the material world) but, rather, a spiritual being.

---

1. Nafisi, 434; Mudarris Razavi, 2: 693, no. 363. Nafisi, 353; Mudarris Razavi, 2: 553, no. 185.
2. Nafisi, 440; Mudarris Razavi, 2: 701, no. 383.

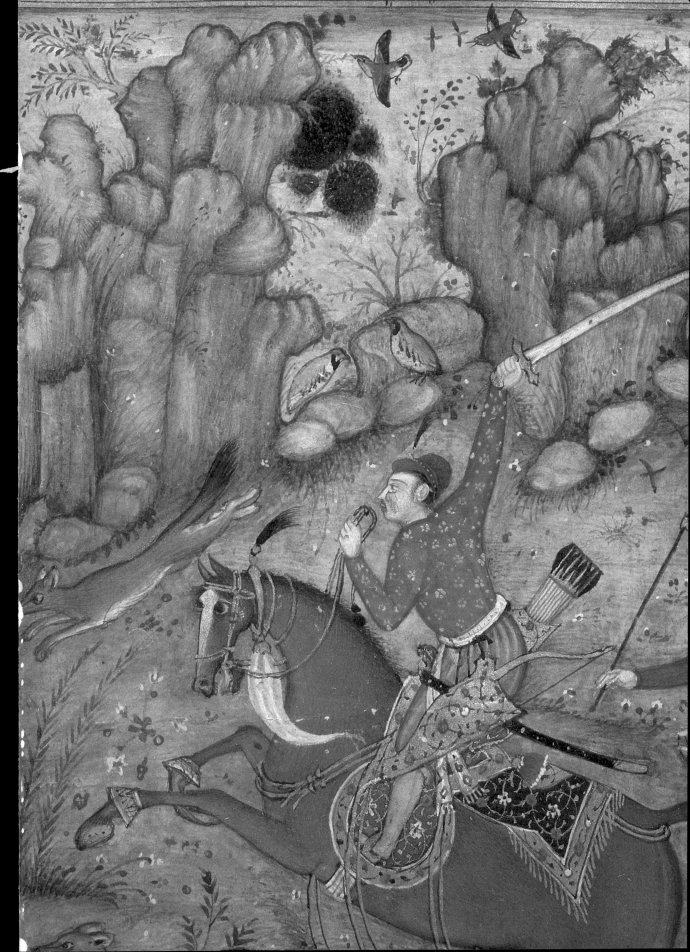

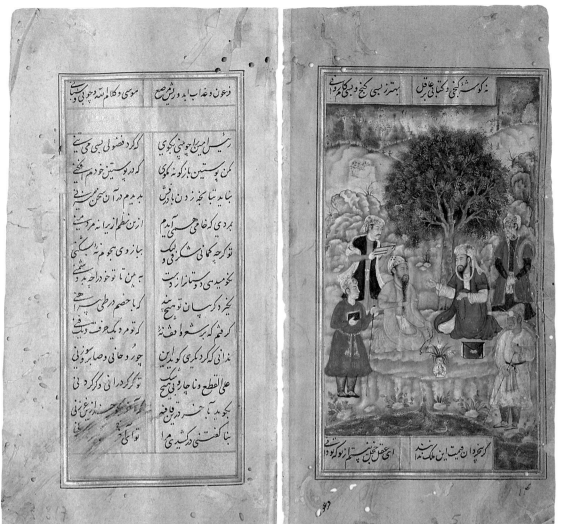

PLATE FOURTEEN

In Praise of the Simple Life

The listener, in his crown and yellow robe, has reacted all too promptly to the wise poet's suggestion and has sprouted Pharaoh's jeweled beard. His "hell," however, is agreeably royal. One wonders whether the figures bearing books have brought them for "a sensitive man," who prefers them to "wealth... and the prosperous life," or whether the bearers are misguided scholars in search of daily bread.

Fol. 316b contains a *qiṭʻa* called "Advice":[1]

> Master, if possible, don't seek a scholar's career,
> For that will keep you in search of your daily bread.
> Let buffoonery be your profession and learn how to sing,
> That you might take your reward from the high and the low.
> Are not a nook and a book for a sensitive man
> Better than wealth and a kingdom and prosperous life?
> If those dull people do not know this property's worth,
> I'm not ashamed of you, reason: *you* know it quite well!
> Look, Pharaoh is in hell, with his gem-studded beard;
> It was Moses, the shepherd, who was kindly addressed by the Lord.

Fol. 317a continues with a satire on one Raʼis Amin.[2]

1. Nafisi, 471; Mudarris Razavi, 2: 751-52, no. 477.
2. Nafisi, 469-70; not included in Mudarris Razavi.

PLATE FIFTEEN

Birds and Lotus

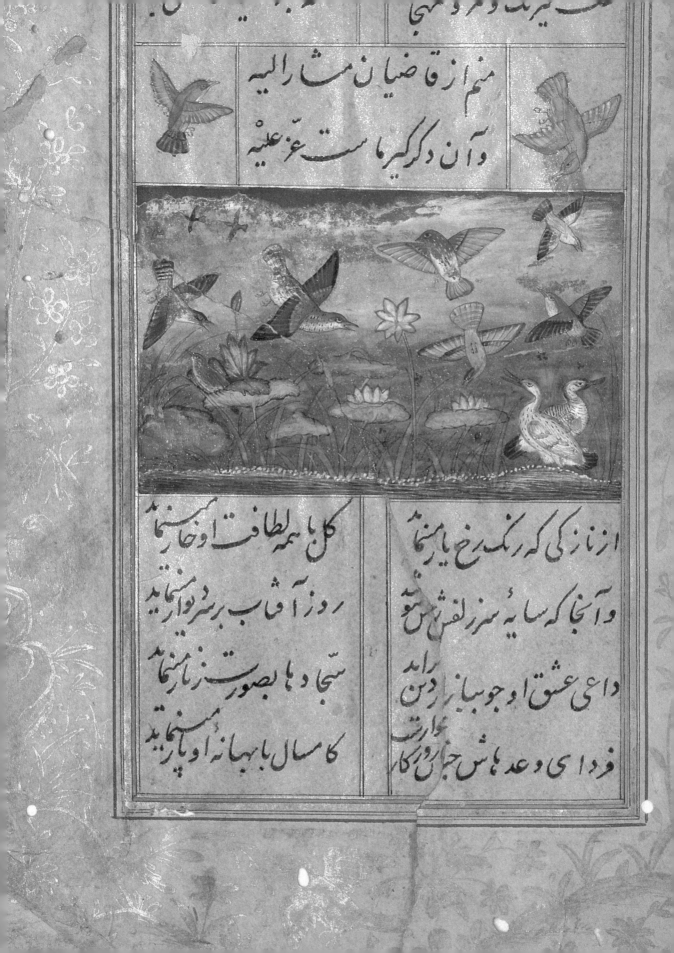

منم از قاضیان مثل الیه

وآن دگر که مراست عز علیه

از نازکی که رنگ رخ یار می‌نما

کل با همه لطافت او خارسنما

وآنجا که سایهٔ سبز زلف نقش من نمود

روز آفتاب بر سر دیوار می‌نما

داعی عشق او و جو بازار دین

سجاده‌ها بصورت زنار می‌نما

فردای وعده هاش جهانی روزگار

کامسال با بهانهٔ او پار می‌نما

The Dīvān's *illustrations end with a pleasurable combination of lotus flowers, rippling water, shoreline, sky, and brightly colored birds. These eager hunters, eyes greedy, beaks sharply open, dip, soar, and dive. Eyecatchingly ornamental, the birds are also believable. Most are foreshortened, caught by the artist "on the wing."*

The previous pages and fol. 336a up to the miniature contain Anvari's only *mathnavī* – a poem in rhyming distichs. Anvari apparently improvised this extremely obscene narrative poem in his youth when Tajuddin 'Amzad of Balkh reviled him for having squandered his inherited fortune. "When he had reached this point [the lines before the miniature on fol. 336a], a group of friends interceded that he might not go further. He left off in order not to offend them."[1]

The miniature marks the division between the *mathnavī* and the lyric *ghazals,* of which Anvari wrote some three hundred. The first one begins on fol. 336b:[2]

The color of my sweetheart's cheek
          seems so transparent that
The roses, tender as they are,
          appear like thorns to me,
And when the shade of his dark curl
          falls, covering his face,
It seems as if the sun at noon
          appears on a white wall.
And when the one who loves him comes
          to the bazaar of faith
All prayer rugs appear as if
          they were a Brahman's thread....

The poet intends to say that all lovers become idolators, adoring the beloved one through whom God's beauty reveals itself.

1. Nafisi, 477-83; not included in Mudarris Razavi.
2. Nafisi, 523; Mudarris Razavi, 2: 852, no. 154.

The last page contains the closing line of a quatrain that shows that the previous page is missing, since the rhyme scheme does not fit. In addition, there are three complete quatrains, the last of which is a blessing for a certain Sayyid (descendant of the Prophet Muhammad) by the name of 'Ali.

The colophon reads:

> *This elegant copy was completed at the hand of the sinful slave who hopes for God's mercy, ...* [name obliterated] – *may God forgive them both* [i.e., the scribe and his father, whose name must have been among the lost words] – *in the city of Lahore at the beginning of Dhu'l-qa'da* 996 [September 22, 1588].

BIBLIOGRAPHY

Abu'l-Fazl. *A'īn i Akbarī.* Trans. H. Blochmann. Calcutta, 1873.

———. *The Akbarnāma.* Trans. H. Beveridge. 3 vols. Calcutta, 1912.

Anvari, Auhaduddin. *Dīvān.* Ed. Muhammad Taqi Mudarris Razavi. Vol. 1, *Qaṣā'id.* Tehran, 1337 sh./A.D. 1958, 2nd, ed., 1347 sh./A.D. 1968. Vol. 2, *Muqaṭṭa'āt, ghazaliyāt, rubā'iyāt.* Tehran, 1340 sh./A.D. 1961.

———. *Dīvān.* Ed. Sa'id-i Nafisi. Tehran, 1337 sh./A.D. 1958.

Arberry, Arthur John. *Classical Persian Poetry.* London, 1958.

Arberry, Arthur John, M. Minovi, B. W. Robinson, and J. V. S. Wilkinson. *The Chester Beatty Library: A Catalogue of the Persian Manuscripts and Miniatures.* 3 vols. Dublin, 1959-62.

'Aufi, Muhammad. *Lubāb al-albāb.* Ed. E. G. Browne and Muhammed Qazvini. London, 1902-4.

Azad Bilgrami. *Khizāna-i 'āmira.* Lucknow, 1871.

Babur. *The Memoirs of Bābur.* Trans. Annette S. Beveridge. 3 fascs. London, 1922.

Al-Badaoni [Abdul Qadir Bin Maluk Shah]. *Muntakhab-ut-Tawārīkh.* Trans. A. Ranking (vol. 1), W. H. Lowe (vol. 2), and T. W. Haig (vol. 3). 3 vols. Calcutta, 1884-1925.

Barrett, Douglas. *Painting of the Deccan, XVI-XVII Century.* London, 1958.

Bayani, Mehdi. "Dīvān-i-Qaṭrān be-khaṭṭ-i Anvarī-i Abīvardī." *Yaghmā* 11/3 (1329 sh./A.D. 1950): 445-74.

Beach, Milo Cleveland. *The Grand Mogul.* Williamstown, Mass., 1978.

Bibliothèque Nationale. Département des manuscrits. *Catalogue des manuscrits persans de la Bibliothèque Nationale.* Vol. 2 of *Catalogue des manuscrits persans par E. Blochet.* Paris, 1905-34.

Binney, Edwin, 3rd. *Indian Miniature Painting from the Collection of Edwin Binney, 3rd.* Portland, Ore., 1974.

Binyon, Laurence, and Thomas Arnold. *Court Painters of the Grand Moguls.* Oxford, 1921.

Brown, Percy. *Indian Painting under the Mughals, A.D. 1550 to A.D. 1750.* Oxford, 1924.

Browne, Edward Granville. *A Literary History of Persia.* 4 vols. Cambridge, 1902; reissue, 1928.

Bucke, Richard Maurice. *Cosmic Consciousness.* New York, 1901.

Catalogue of the Arabic and Persian Manuscripts in the Oriental Public Library at Bankipore. 26 vols. Calcutta, 1908-46.

Chandra, Moti. *The Technique of Mughal Painting.* Lucknow, 1946.

Chandra, Pramod. *The Ṭuṭi-Nāma of the Cleveland Museum of Art,* with facsimile plates of the manuscript. Graz, 1976.

Dickson, Martin Bernard, and Stuart Cary Welch. *The Houghton Shahnameh.* 2 vols. Cambridge, Mass., 1981.

Ethé, Hermann. "Neupersische Literatur." In *Grundriss der iranischen Philologie.* Ed. Wilhelm Geiger and Ernst Kuhn, 2: 212-370. Strasbourg, 1898-1902.

Fouchécour, C. H. de. *La Description de la nature dans la poésie lyrique persane du XIIème siècle.* Paris, 1969.

Gascoigne, Bamber. *The Great Moghuls.* London, 1971.

Glück, Heinrich. *Die indischen Miniaturen des Haemzae-romanes....* Zurich, 1925.

Goethe, Johann-Wolfgang von. *West-Oestlicher Divan.* Stuttgart, 1819.

Gray, Basil. "Painting." In *Art of India and Pakistan, a Commemorative Catalogue of the Exhibition Held at the Royal Academy of Arts, London, 1947-8.* London, 1950.

Gul-Badan, Begam (Princess Rose Body). *The History of Humāyūn.* Trans. Annette S. Beveridge. London, 1902.

Hammer-Purgstall, Joseph von. *Geschichte der schönen Redekünste Persiens.* Vienna, 1818.

Hamza-nāma: Dāstān-i Amīr Ḥamza. Ed. Gerhart Egger. Graz, 1974.

Hendley, Thomas H. *Memorials of the Jeypore Exhibition 1883.* 4 vols. London, 1883.

Hutchins, Francis G. *Young Krishna.* West Franklin, N.H., 1980.

Irvine, William. *The Army of the Indian Moghuls.* London, 1903.

Ivanov, A. A., T. V. Grek, and O. F. Akimushkin. *Al'bom indiyskikh i persiskikh miniatyur XVI-XVIII vv.* (The Album of Indian and Persian Miniatures of the 16th-18th Centuries). Moscow, 1962.

Jahangir. *The Tūzuk-i Jahāngīrī; or Memoirs of Jahāngīr.* Trans. Alexander Rogers. Ed. Henry Beveridge. 2 vols. London, 1909-14.

Jami. *Bahāristan.* Lucknow, 1875.

Kirkpatrick, William. "The Tears of Khorassan." In *The Asiatic Miscellany.* Calcutta, 1785.

Köprülüzade, Mehmet Fuat. *Eski Şairlerimiz: Divan edebiyatı antolojisi.* Istanbul, 1931.

Kühnel, Ernst, and Hermann Goetz. *Indian Book Painting from Jahangir's Album in the State Library in Berlin.* London, 1926.

Levy, Reuben. *Persian Literature. An Introduction.* London, 1923.

Martin, F. R. *The Miniature Painting and Painters of Persia, India, and Turkey from the 8th to the 18th Century.* 2 vols. London, 1912.

Moynihan, Elizabeth A. *Paradise as a Garden in Persia and Mughal India.* New York, 1979.

Nasim, K. B. "The Life and Works of Ḥakīm Auḥad-ud-Dīn Anwarī." *Journal of the Arabic and Persian Society of the Punjab University,* 10-11 (1965-66): 1-346.

Nizam ud-Din Ahmad. *Ṭabaqāt-i Akbari.* Trans. B. De. 2 vols. Calcutta, 1913-36.

Nizami 'Arudi. *Chahār Maqāla.* Ed. Muhammed Qazvini. London, 1910. Text and commentary in Persian.

————. *Revised Translation of the Chahār Maqāla ("Four Discourses") of Nizāmī-i-Arūḍī.* Trans. E. G. Browne. London, 1921.

Pagliaro, Antonio, and Alessandro Bausani. *Storia della letteratura persiana.* Milan, 1960.

Pope, Arthur Upham, ed. *A Survey of Persian Art from Prehistoric Times to the Present.* 6 vols. Oxford, 1938-39.

Prashad, Beni. *History of Jahangir.* 3d. ed. Allahabad, 1940.

Rizvi, Saiyid Athar Abbas, and Vincent Adams Flynn. *Fatḥpur-Sīkrī.* Bombay, 1975.

Rumi, Jalaluddin Maulana. *Dīvān-i kabīr.* Ed. Badi 'uzzaman Furuzanfar. 10 vols. Tehran, 1336 sh./A.D. 1957.

————. *Mathnawī-i Ma'nawī.* Ed. and trans. Reynold A. Nicholson. 8 vols. London, 1925-40.

Rypka, Jan. *History of Iranian Literature.* Dordrecht, Netherlands, 1968.

Sa'dī. *Gulistān.* From the manuscript of Muhammad 'Ali Furughi. Tehran, 1342 sh./A.D. 1963.

Samsam-ud-Daula (Shah Nawaz Khan) and 'Abdul Hayy. *The Maāthir-ul-Umarā.* Trans. H. Beveridge and Beni Prashad. 2 vols. Calcutta, 1911-52.

Schimmel, Annemarie. *Mystical Dimensions of Islam.* Chapel Hill, N.C., 1975.

Shahidi, Ja'far. *Sharh-i lughāt va mushkilāt-i Dīvān-i Anvarī Abīvardī.* Tehran 1357 sh./A.D. 1978.

Shiveshwarkar, Leela. *The Pictures of the Chaurapañchāśikā, a Sanskrit Love Lyric.* New Delhi, 1967.

Shyam, Radhey. *The Kingdom of Ahmadnagar.* Delhi, 1966.

Simsar, Muhammad A. *The Cleveland Museum of Art's Ṭuṭi-Nāma/Tales of a Parrot.* Graz, 1978.

Skelton, Robert. "Mughal Painting from the Harivamsá." In *Victoria and Albert Museum Yearbook, Number 2.* London, 1969.

Smith, Vincent Arthur. *Akbar the Great Mogul, 1542-1605.* 2d. rev. ed. Oxford, 1919.

Spear, Percival. *India: A Modern History.* Ann Arbor, 1961.

Stchoukine, Ivan V. *Les Miniatures indiennes.* Paris, 1929.

Titley, Norah M. *Miniatures from Persian Manuscripts.* London, 1977.

Welch, Stuart Cary. *The Art of Mughal India.* New York, 1964.

_____. *A Flower from Every Meadow.* New York, 1973.

_____. *Imperial Mughal Painting.* New York, 1978.

_____. *Indian Drawings and Painted Sketches.* New York, 1976.

_____. *A King's Book of Kings: The Shahnameh of Shah Tahmasp.* New York, 1972.

_____. *Persian Paintings: Five Royal Safavid Manuscripts of the Sixteenth Century.* New York, 1976.

Zhukovski, Valentine. *Materials for a Biography and Characteristic Sketch; 'Alī Awḥadu' d-Din Anwarī.* St. Petersburg, 1883.

INDEX OF PROPER NAMES

INDEX OF MANUSCRIPTS
AND LITERARY TERMS